Warrior • 120

Hittite Warrior

Trevor Bryce • Illustrated by Adam Hook

First published in Great Britain in 2007 by Osprey Publishing,
Midland House, West Way, Botley, Oxford OX2 0PH, UK
44-02 23rd St, Suite 219, Long Island City, NY 11101, USA
Email: info@ospreypublishing.com

Transferred to digital print on demand 2010

First published 2007
2nd impression 2008

Printed and bound by PrintOnDemand-Worldwide.com, Peterborough, UK

A CIP catalogue record for this book is available from the British Library

ISBN: 978 1 84603 081 9

Page layout by Scribe, Oxford.
Index by Alan Thatcher
Maps by John Richards
Originated by PDQ Digital Media Solutions
Typeset in Helvetica Neue and ITC New Baskerville

Glossary

arzana	A house of entertainment
BEL MADGALTI	'Lord of the Watchtower'
GAL MESHEDI	'Chief of the Bodyguards'
LÚ ^{GIŠ}**TUKUL**	'Man of the Weapon' – civilians sometimes called up for military service
MESHEDI	The Hittite king's most prestigious bodyguards
UKU.UŠ	Professional standing army troops

Artist's note

Readers may care to note that the original paintings from which the colour plates in this book were prepared are available for
private sale. All reproduction copyright whatsoever is retained by the Publisher. Enquiries should be addressed to:

Adam Hook
Scorpio Gallery
PO Box 475
Hailsham
East Sussex
BN27 2SL
UK

The Publishers regret that they can enter into no correspondence upon this matter.

The Woodland Trust

Osprey Publishing is supporting the Woodland Trust, the UK's leading woodland conservation charity, by funding the
dedication of trees.

www.ospreypublishing.com

CONTENTS

HITTITE WARRIOR

INTRODUCTION

Some 3,700 years ago, at the dawn of the Late Bronze Age, a kingdom arose in central Anatolia (modern Turkey), which became one of the great superpowers of the ancient Near Eastern world. It was called the kingdom of Hatti. Today, we refer to the inhabitants of this land as the Hittites. In their own day, the Hittites simply called themselves the people of the Land of Hatti. From their royal capital Hattusa, the rulers of Hatti embarked on a programme of territorial expansion that took their armies westwards across the face of Anatolia to the Aegean Sea, south-eastwards through northern Syria and then across the Euphrates river into Mesopotamia. In the 14th and 13th centuries BC, the Hittites controlled the most powerful empire of the Late Bronze Age. By the 1320s BC, under their warlord emperor Suppiluliuma, they had destroyed their most dangerous rival, the kingdom of Mitanni. Egypt, Babylon and Assyria were the other great powers of the age. Their rulers formed with Suppiluliuma a kind of elite, highly exclusive club. They corresponded regularly with one another, exchanged gifts and addressed one another as 'My Brother'

General view from the south of the Hittite capital Hattusa, with recently excavated temples in the foreground. On the rising ground behind them, the royal palace, built on the city's acropolis, is highlighted by sunlight.

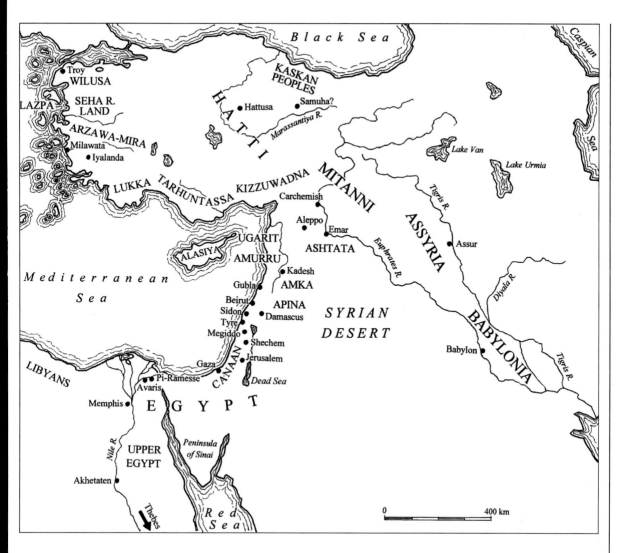

The following labels appear on the map:

Black Sea · Caspian Sea · Troy · WILUSA · KASKAN PEOPLES · Hattusa · Samuha? · SEHA R. LAND · HATTI · LAZPA · ARZAWA-MIRA · Milawata · Iyalanda · *Marassantiya R.* · Lake Van · Lake Urmia · LUKKA · TARHUNTASSA · KIZZUWADNA · MITANNI · Carchemish · *Tigris R.* · Aleppo · Emar · ASHTATA · ASSYRIA · Assur · UGARIT · *Euphrates R.* · ALASIYA · AMURRU · *Diyala R.* · Kadesh · Gubla · AMKA · *Mediterranean Sea* · Beirut · APINA · Babylon · Sidon · Damascus · BABYLONIA · Tyre · SYRIAN DESERT · Megiddo · Shechem · *Tigris R.* · Gaza · Jerusalem · CANAAN · Pi-Ramesse · Dead Sea · Avaris · LIBYANS · Memphis · EGYPT · *Nile R.* · UPPER EGYPT · Peninsula of Sinai · Akhetaten · Thebes · *Red Sea* · 0 400 km

and 'Great King'. But their diplomatic communications, their often lavish gifts, their marriage unions and their profuse expressions of mutual love and devotion barely concealed their distrust of one another and the underlying tensions in their relationships, which sometimes erupted into open conflict.

The Great King of Hatti held sway over a large array of subject territories, which extended over much of Anatolia, and in Syria reached as far south as the city of Damascus. In the Damascus region, Hatti shared a frontier with Egypt. The subject territories consisted largely of vassal and protectorate states, each controlled by a local ruler bound by treaty to his Hittite overlord. Many treaties have survived. They spell out the local ruler's obligations to the Hittite king, including his military obligations. In return, the Hittite king guaranteed his support for the ruler and his legitimate successors, promising military assistance whenever the need arose. King Suppiluliuma also established viceregal kingdoms at Aleppo and Carchemish in Syria. Carchemish, on the Euphrates river, had formerly been a stronghold of the Mitannian empire. Each viceregal kingdom was ruled by a member of the Hittite royal family, generally the son of the reigning king.

Map of the Near Eastern world in the Late Bronze Age.

The acropolis today. The well-preserved foundations of the acropolis building were unearthed by a succession of German archaeological teams last century.

Hittite kings used diplomacy as an extremely important tool in managing their empire. It was exercised primarily through sworn pacts, which the kings drew up with their subject rulers and their royal peers, and through regular exchanges of letters with foreign and vassal courts. But diplomacy on its own could not guarantee lasting peace within the Hittite empire. In fact, the fortunes of the Hittites waxed and waned dramatically throughout their 500-year history, and several times their kingdom teetered on the brink of annihilation. The Hittite homeland, the core region in central Anatolia of the kingdom of Hatti, was landlocked, and surrounded by enemies. Hostile neighbours were ever ready to exploit any perceived weakening in Hittite power or instability in the monarchy by crossing the homeland's frontiers, sacking and occupying its territories and cities and, at least once, capturing and sacking the capital.

A highly efficient fighting force was essential to the building of the Hittite empire, and also to the defence of the realm against its many enemies, who threatened to dismember and engulf it.

CHRONOLOGY

Note: all dates are approximate and BC.

Early 17th century Foundation of Hittite Old Kingdom.
1650–1620 Hattusili I makes Hattusa the Hittite royal capital, conquers large parts of Anatolia and campaigns in northern Syria and across the Euphrates.
1620–1590 Mursili I succeeds his grandfather Hattusili, and conquers Aleppo in Syria and Babylon in Mesopotamia.

Suppiluliuma I, as depicted in the docu-drama *The Hittites*. He was the greatest of all Hittite warrior-kings. During his reign in the 14th century BC, the kingdom of Hatti became the supreme political and military power in the Near Eastern world. (Courtesy Ekip Film)

1590–1525 Mursili is assassinated. The Hittite kingdom is weakened by succession struggles. Enemy forces invade the homeland.

1525–1500 Telipinu seizes the throne, stabilizes the monarchy and regains some of the Hittites' lost territories.

1500–1400 Weakness and division in the kingdom under a succession of ineffective rulers. In northern Mesopotamia and Syria, the Hurrian kingdom of Mitanni emerges.

1400–1350 Foundation of Hittite New Kingdom. Hatti reasserts its authority as an international power, with military campaigns in Anatolia and Syria. Massive enemy attacks on its homeland, however, almost destroy the kingdom. Hattusa is abandoned and sacked.

1350–1322 King Tudhaliya III and his son Suppiluliuma regain the kingdom. Suppiluliuma becomes king and conducts military campaigns in Syria and Mesopotamia. He destroys the kingdom of Mitanni.

1322–1295 Suppiluliuma and his son and successor Arnuwanda die of plague. Arnuwanda's brother Mursili II becomes king, and establishes his authority throughout the kingdom. Assyria becomes a major power in Mesopotamia.

1295–1272 Muwattalli II succeeds his father Mursili and transfers the Hittite capital to Tarhuntassa in southern Anatolia. In 1274 he fights Ramesses II in the battle of Kadesh. The battle ends inconclusively, but the Hittites pursue the Egyptians south, occupying Syrian territory north of Damascus.

1272–1237 Urhi-Teshub succeeds his father Muwattalli and restores Hattusa as the capital. He is overthrown by his uncle Hattusili in a civil war. Hattusili (III) becomes king and concludes a treaty with Ramesses in 1269.

1237–1209 The kingdom is now in decline, and under Hattusili's son and successor Tudhaliya IV, the Hittites are defeated by the Assyrians in a battle in northern Mesopotamia.

1209–early 12th century Under its last two rulers, the kingdom continues to decline until its final collapse. Yet under the last king, Suppiluliuma II, the Hittites engage in naval warfare, off the coast of Cyprus, for the first known time in their history, and are victorious.

Hatti's fall is due to a combination of factors, including attacks by bands of marauders and tribes from the mountains north of the homeland, internal upheavals and prolonged food shortages.

List of Hittite Kings

Old Kingdom

1650:	Labarna
1650–1620:	Hattusili I (grandson?)
1620–1590:	Mursili I (grandson, adopted son)
1590–1560:	Hantili I (brother-in-law)
	Zidanta I (son-in-law)
1560–1525:	Ammuna (son)
	Huzziya I (brother of Ammuna's daughter-in-law)
1525–1500:	Telipinu (brother-in-law)
	Aluwamna (son-in-law)
	Tahurwaili (interloper)
1500–1400:	Hantili II (son of Alluwamna?)
	Zidanta II (son?)
	Huzziya II (son?)
	Muwattalli I (interloper)

New Kingdom

	Tudhaliya I/II (grandson of Huzziya II?)
1400–1350:	Arnuwanda I[1] (son-in-law, adopted son)
	Hattusili II? (son?)
	Tudhaliya III (son?)
1350–1322:	Suppiluliuma I (son)
1322–1321:	Arnuwanda II (son)
1321–1295:	Mursili II (brother)
1295–1272:	Muwattalli II (son)
1272–1267:	Urhi-Teshub (son)
1267–1237:	Hattusili III (uncle)
1237–1228:	Tudhaliya IV (son)
1228–1227:	Karunta[2] (cousin)
1227–1209:	Tudhaliya IV[3] (cousin)
1209–1207:	Arnuwanda III (son)
1207:	Suppiluliuma II (brother)

1. Includes period of co-regency
2. Conjectural Great King of Hatti
3. 2nd period as king?

Note: All dates are approximate. Sequential reigns are grouped when it is impossible to suggest even approximate dates for individual kings.

THE HIERARCHY OF COMMAND

Who were the troops making up the Hittite army, where did they come from and how were they recruited? The Great King himself was commander-in-chief of the army. He spent part of almost every year on military campaigns, often in regions far from the homeland. Prowess in war was an essential part of the ideology of kingship. A king was expected to prove himself in battle, and to equal, and if possible surpass, his predecessors' military exploits. Hence his need to conduct campaigns in person – not only to defend his realm but also to maintain his credibility among his own subjects, and to ensure his troops' loyalty by bestowing upon them a share of the spoils of conquest. He had also to demonstrate his military prowess to his enemies, who were quick to seize upon a new king's inexperience as a war leader to attack and plunder his lands. The young king Mursili II, for example, who found himself upon the throne after the sudden death of his father and elder brother, was treated with contempt by the kingdom's enemies:

> You are a child; you know nothing and instil no fear in me. Your land is now in ruins, your infantry and chariotry are few. Against your infantry, I have many infantry; against your chariotry, I have many chariotry. Your father had many infantry and chariotry. But you, who are a child, how can you match him?[1]

Because of their vulnerability, particular attention was given to training future kings from an early age in the techniques and skills of warfare. On at least two occasions, crown princes received their battlefield initiation in their early teens. The later king Tudhaliya IV was given command of a Hittite army when he was only 14.

The king himself may sometimes have led his troops into the thick of battle, with 'his gods running before him', and on occasions may have engaged in hand-to-hand fighting with the enemy. We know of no case, however, where a Hittite king was killed in action, though one of the early kings may have died of battle wounds. In most cases, the king probably directed operations from a vantage point safely removed from the thick of the fray, or was at least surrounded by his bodyguard in the battle's midst. Hittite pragmatism would have seen to it that the king, or his heir designate, was not too closely exposed to the hazards of battle. The possibility that a well-directed enemy shaft, or a lucky sword thrust, could in an instant plunge the kingdom into crisis was an unacceptable risk.

There were occasions when a king could not take personal command of an army; for example, if he were involved in a military operation elsewhere, or had other pressing matters to attend to – including the performance of neglected religious duties. In these cases, he could delegate military command to a subordinate, probably a member of his own family. The king's brothers often seem to have been appointed to high military commands

Seal impression of the king Mursili II. Documents were validated by the seals of kings and royal officials. On this seal impression, we see two rings of cuneiform ('wedge-shaped') signs indicating Mursili's name, titles and ancestry. The inner circle contains hieroglyphic symbols, which read 'Great King', surmounted by a winged sun-disk – a symbol of royalty borrowed from Egypt.

1. Extract from *Annals of Mursili II [Die Annales des Mursilis]*.

The king departs on a military campaign. He probably led his troops from the city through the so-called King's Gate, after praying for success against his enemies at a chapel just inside the gate. His robe and headband distinguish him from the rest of his forces. (Courtesy Ekip Film)

immediately below the king and the crown prince, particularly if they held the highly prestigious post of *GAL MESHEDI* (Chief of the Bodyguards). Other officers, usually of princely status, bore the titles Chief of the Chariot-Warriors of the Right, Chief of the Chariot-Warriors of the Left, Chief of the Standing Army-Troops of the Right, Chief of the Standing Army-Troops of the Left, and Chiefs of the 'Shepherds' of the Right and Left.[2] Each of these officers apparently commanded a brigade of 1,000 men.

Other members of the Hittite nobility were assigned military commands, sometimes as divisional commanders within an army under the leadership of the king or a prince, sometimes as the leaders of smaller-scale military expeditions sent against an enemy or a rebel vassal state. When given an independent command, a military leader could exercise considerable initiative in terms of strategies and battle tactics. He was, however, obliged to report directly to the king on all aspects of his military operations, and could be rebuked or severely punished by the king for incompetence. Even when he was not leading a campaign, the king closely monitored all aspects of it through regular exchange of messages and bulletins with the field commander.

The lower-ranking officers included, in descending order of importance, 'overseers of military heralds', 'dignitaries', and 'gentlemen'. There was a gradation of rank within the dignitaries category, ranging (in modern equivalents) from captain to sergeant. The gentlemen were the lowest-ranking officers. Each officer's importance was determined by the number of men he led. At the lower levels, some were in charge of 100 men, some of just ten.

---

2. See R. H. Beal, 'Hittite Military Organization', in J. M. Sasson (ed.), *Civilizations of the Ancient Near East*, 4 vols (New York, 1995), pp.546–47.

ENLISTMENT

Hittite texts are not very helpful for attempts to calculate the size of the Hittite military forces. Obviously, the size of the force varied, depending on the nature of the military operation. We have some figures for troops who took part in sieges; the size of a siege-force was governed by the size of the besieged city and the strength of its fortifications and defending force. A text dating back a century or so before the Hittite period records the siege of the city of Hattus, predecessor of the Hittite capital Hattusa. Hattus was a small city, with a population of perhaps no more than 5,000, but it is likely that a force of at least 1,500 infantry and 50 to 100 chariots would have been needed to breach its fortifications and capture it. Investment of larger cities like Carchemish in the Hittite period probably required a substantially greater besieging force. Expeditionary units dispatched against rebellious vassals or hostile independent states likely numbered between 5,000 and 10,000 troops, depending on the strength of the enemy, the support they had from other states in the region and the extent to which the Hittites could call upon assistance from loyal vassals in the region. For a major engagement against another great king, the Hittites undoubtedly put a much larger force into the field. In the battle of Kadesh, Ramesses tells us that the Hittite forces numbered 47,500, including 3,500 chariotry and 37,000 infantry. This figure is probably not exaggerated. The Hittite king drew heavily on all available resources for his showdown with Egypt, including contingents from far-flung parts of his realm, and an unknown number of mercenaries. An international conflict on this scale involved tens of thousands of infantry and chariotry.

Throughout their history the Hittites were faced with chronic manpower shortages, particularly evident when a major Hittite campaign was conducted against an enemy far from the homeland. Such a campaign seriously depleted the homeland's defence capabilities, and often prompted hostile forces to sweep across the homeland's inadequately defended frontiers. The situation became all the more serious when the Hittites had to conduct simultaneous campaigns in different regions. Further, when the need arose to bring forces up to maximum strength, this meant levying the population at large, and consequently calling up farmers employed in the vital role of producing food for the Hittite state. When men of yeoman stock were needed for military service, it was best to summon them at times in the year when agricultural activity was least intensive, avoiding sowing and harvesting periods. The campaigning season was generally limited to the period from spring to autumn, to avoid the winter snows, but there was no guarantee that crises requiring a full-scale call-up could be confined to agriculturally quiet periods.

Hittite kings usually sought to resolve crises by means other than military conflict – hence the importance attached to resolution by diplomacy rather than brute force. When military confrontation was deemed unavoidable, a king had to use his available resources economically and efficiently, taking every opportunity to supplement these resources with reinforcements from his vassal or allied states in or near the campaign area.

As we have seen, the highest ranks in the army were held by members of the royal family. None were full-time soldiers. The king himself was not only his kingdom's war-leader, but also its supreme judicial authority and chief priest. So too his sons, brothers and other members of his family combined military roles with judicial, religious and administrative responsibilities. Many of the nobility who provided the king with his officer class had other roles as well. At least some of them constituted a kind of land-owning aristocracy. They owned rural estates where crops and orchards were grown and livestock raised, and joined the king for military campaigns on a seasonal basis. Much of their land may have come to them as a grant from the king – a reward for their past loyalty or to ensure their future loyalty. A major incentive for serving in the army was that they received a substantial part of the booty from each campaign, in the form of sheep, cattle and prisoners-of-war, which they used to restock their estates. Military duties constituted but one part of a range of responsibilities exercised by the king's provincial governors, particularly in the outlying districts of the homeland territories.

The Pharaoh Ramesses II, from Ramesses' temple at Abu Simbel in Lower Nubia. The sculpture is one of four colossal seated figures of the king that flank the entrance to the temple.

The lower levels of the officer class would have been made up of career soldiers. Indeed, the core of the defence force was a full-time, professional standing army. The troops in this army were perenially on duty, liable to be called on at any time to fight for king and country. They lived together in military barracks, so that they could be mobilized at a moment's notice. The majority were probably quartered in Hattusa, particularly during winter. In practice, their fighting role was confined to the campaigning season, but since they were full-time employees of the state, they had to be provided with rations for the whole of the year. Hence the state ensured that in the 'off-season' the soldiers were gainfully employed in other ways.

Almost certainly, many if not the majority of full-time soldiers were volunteers from within the homeland who sought to make the army a career, with the various rewards as well as the risks that soldiering offered. The standing army, however, was recruited from other sources as well, most notably from the kingdom's subject territories. The king required provincial districts within his realm to provide a certain number of recruits for his standing army. These were sent to Hattusa where they were quartered in the military barracks and began their life as professional soldiers. Apparently it was up to the local authorities of each district to decide who would be chosen for what must have been a very dubious honour for many recruits. The king stipulated that none of the recruits could be slaves, nor could they be substitutes for any who had originally been selected and had tried to avoid military service by bribing others to take their place.

Soldiers of the standing army. They are in the midst of a military campaign and are waiting to receive the day's orders from their immediate superior, the lowest-ranking Hittite officer who commanded a group of ten. Two types of helmet are shown, metal and leather. Both types are depicted in relief sculptures of Hittite warriors. (Courtesy Ekip Film)

Conscripts from a particular district were kept together in Hattusa, and quartered in the same barracks. The unit in which they served and the barracks where they were quartered were named after the province or district from which they came, and apparently they served under an officer recruited from the same region. This system may have been for morale-building purposes, or to promote close bonding within a particular military unit. It may also have served an important practical purpose. Many languages were spoken throughout the Hittite empire, and for training and effective communication of orders it was no doubt important to keep together groups of men with the same regional language.

Almost certainly, the king's standing army was also made up partly of adult males transported to the Hittite homeland from conquered countries as prisoners-of-war. While the king allocated a number of these transportees to his officers, he kept a large proportion of them for his own service. Some were assigned duties in the homeland's temples, some were sent to build up the population of frontier settlements and others were pressed into service in the army. The system became a major mechanism for replenishment for the homeland's agricultural workforce as well as the ranks of the military. Our earliest reference to it is in the Annals of the early 14th-century king Tudhaliya. After a successful campaign in western Anatolia, Tudhaliya took from the region 10,000 infantry and 600 teams of horse, along with the elite chariot contingent, the so-called 'lords of the bridle'. He brought them all to Hattusa for resettlement – perhaps in an underpopulated part of the homeland – and placed them under the command of one of their own leaders, Kukkulli, who had also been transported back to Hattusa. On this occasion, however, the policy of keeping transportees together under a commander from their own region backfired, as Kukkulli stirred his countrymen to rebellion. The rebellion was promptly crushed, and Kukkulli was killed.

Clearly there were risks in not promptly dispersing groups of prisoners from a conquered state. No doubt this particular episode led to more stringent safeguards and tighter control over such groups. But there were obvious advantages in selecting, for a permanent standing army, conscripts from conquered countries in their physical prime, experienced in battle and fierce-spirited. For this reason, some of the standing army was made up of recruits from one of the most formidable peoples confronting the Hittites throughout their history. These were tribesmen from the land of Kaska, which occupied the mountainous Pontic region along the southern shores of the Black Sea, north of the Hittite homeland. Able-bodied males from this land who had peacefully settled in Hittite territory were recruited by Hattusili III as standing troops for the army. Hattusili had direct experience of their fighting qualities, and apparently welcomed the opportunity to harness these qualities for his own forces. He did not altogether trust them, however. They were kept under close supervision, and had limitations imposed on their movements, including a ban on entering a city in the territory where they were quartered.

In the peak period of the empire, the Hittite standing army was probably some tens of thousands strong. Generally, this was a sufficient force to maintain order and security throughout the empire. Yet when a king had to mount campaigns on two or more fronts, received news of widespread uprisings in the vassal states, or was threatened by a powerful foreign ruler, it was time for a general levy of the Hittite male population, to swell the ranks of the professional army. Troops were called up from the various homeland regions as well as from the vassal states and other subject territories.

A double-headed eagle, symbol of Hittite military power. The relief appears by the entrance of the Hittite city now known as Alaca Höyük. Its Hittite name may have been Arinna.

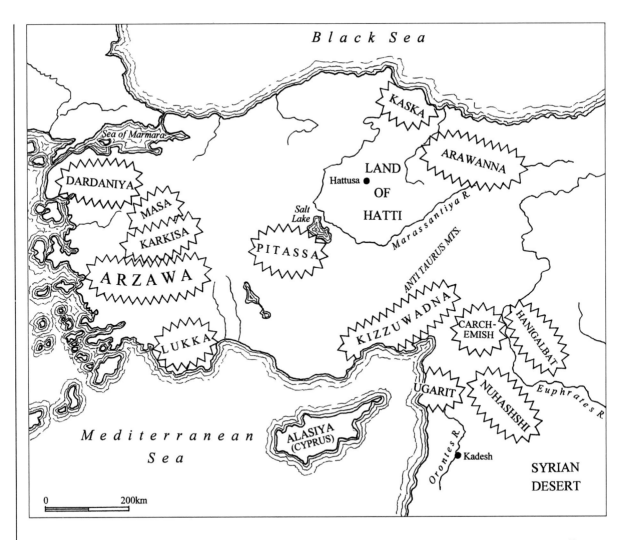

Map showing areas of Hittite recruitment for Kadesh.

The civilians drafted for military service were not necessarily raw recruits. Some already possessed skills that could be used to good effect on the battlefield. They were assigned roles in the army on the basis of these skills. Some were made archers, and others assigned to the chariot corps. However, the bulk of civilian recruits were enlisted in the infantry and in some cases assigned to garrison duties.

Between the professional full-time troops and the civilian-soldiers called up for occasional military service, there was a category of 'reservists'. In Hittite, the term *LÚ* ^{GIŠ}*TUKUL*, which literally means 'Man of the Weapon', was probably first used to apply to such part-time soldiers (the ^{GIŠ} indicates that the weapons in question were originally made of wood). These men were almost certainly better trained than the civilian soldiers. They could be assembled promptly, and probably on a fairly regular basis, for service in the army during the campaigning season. Their payment was in the form of land assigned to them by the king. Its produce was supposed to support them and their families throughout the year. Thus, unlike the full-time soldier, they did not spend their lives in military barracks, and could enjoy a normal family life until king and country called upon them. The king was thus spared the expense of feeding, sheltering and housing them all year round. Such an arrangement no doubt had its problems, since soldier-farmers must often have been away on campaign precisely when their farms most needed their attention or supervision. Additionally, the unsettling effects of dividing one's time between the excitement and unpredictability of military campaigns and the often tedious routine of farming life would hardly have been conducive to maintaining a stable productive agricultural workforce. The system of paying troops with allotments of land may have been abolished or considerably scaled down early in Hittite history, but it was extended to other forms of employment in the king's service. Anyone paid in this way continued to be called a 'Man of the Weapon', even after the term had lost its military connotations.

Mercenaries were recruited from time to time, though probably only when the king needed to muster a larger than normal fighting force to confront a powerful adversary. The best known example of the use of mercenaries is in the battle of Kadesh. According to Ramesses:

> the Wretched Fallen One at Kadesh [i.e. the Hittite king Muwattalli] left no silver in the land. He stripped it of all its possessions, and gave them to all the foreign countries in order to bring them with him to fight.[3]

Ramesses is almost certainly talking about the mercenary troops that the Hittites brought to Kadesh, and he exaggerates their role in the conflict. Even so, a number of the contingents of troops listed on the Hittite side in the battle did come from countries independent of Hittite control, and may have been at Kadesh purely as mercenaries.

CLOTHING AND EQUIPMENT

Dress

On the inside of one of the three main gates of Hattusa, an adult male figure is carved, almost 2m (6ft 6in.) in height and kitted out for war. He wears a helmet, apparently made of leather, with a long plume, cheek and neck flaps, and a short kilt belted at the waist. The kilt, probably also of leather, is decorated with incised registers of interlocking spirals and diagonal straight lines. The warrior's upper torso is bare. From it sprouts a crop of wiry hair. Long hair flows down the warrior's back from beneath his helmet. In some depictions of Hittite warriors, the hair descends behind the neck in a thick plait. Perhaps the fashion of letting the hair grow long was intended to give warriors extra protection against arrows, spear thrusts and sword slashes from the rear. In his right hand, the warrior carries a battle-axe. At his left side, a sword with curved blade is tucked into his belt. His legs below his knees are protected by greaves.

A relief sculpture of a warrior god almost 2m (6ft 6in.) high depicted on the inner side of the King's Gate at Hattusa. His left hand is clenched, perhaps as a victory gesture as he bids farewell to the king and his troops on their departure from Hattusa for a military campaign.

3. Excerpt from Kadesh Inscription, see A. Gardiner, *The Kadesh Inscriptions of Ramesses II* (Oxford, 1975), p.8.

His raised left arm terminates in a clenched fist. The gate on which this figure appears is commonly known as the King's Gate, for it was long thought to depict a Hittite king departing for war. However, it is almost certainly a Hittite god in warrior garb – probably the god Sharrumma, patron deity of King Tudhaliya IV (c.1237–1209), in whose reign the figure was carved. His raised left arm and clenched fist may represent a victory salute to the king as he leads his troops from Hattusa at the beginning of a campaign.

What we see is probably the basic kit of a Hittite soldier on campaign. That a god should be so represented is appropriate, for Hittite kings believed that their gods literally accompanied them on the march, and ran before them into battle. For a warrior, the figure wears surprisingly little in the way of protective armour, though it has been suggested, implausibly, that the chest-hair should be interpreted as part of a shirt of mail. Another depiction of a warrior figure found in the Hittite capital has a well-clad upper torso. The warrior in this case survives in fragmentary form and has been incised on the inside of a broken ceramic bowl. He too wears a helmet with cheek and neck flaps, and has a long plume attached to the back of his helmet. But the helmet itself is much more elaborate than that worn by the warrior-god. It is decorated on its surface with registers of diagonal lines (like those on the kilt of the warrior-god), has a figure-9-shaped crest and a horn-shaped protuberance. The warrior wears a jacket, decorated with a pattern of concentric circles and with sleeves reaching just below the elbows. This jacket may have covered a shirt of scale-armour. Unfortunately, we cannot be sure if the figure we have been describing was in fact a Hittite warrior. The piece of pottery depicting him shows only part of the original composition, and he may have been an enemy from the Aegean world, in combat with a Hittite warrior now lost

A rear view of a bronze statuette of a Hittite warrior wearing a thick plait descending down his back. The plait was probably designed to give some protection to the warrior against an attack from his rear. (© Photo RMN – Statuette of Hittite Warrior, Paris, Louvre Museum)

A warrior depicted on a pottery fragment discovered in the Hittite capital. It is possible that the figure is of western Anatolian or Aegean origin. (From K. Bittel, 'Tonschale mit Ritzzeichung von Boğazköy', *Revue Archéologique* 1, 1976, 9–14, © PUF 1976)

to us. The scale-armour was certainly a standard part of a Hittite warrior's protective covering, for pieces of such armour have been unearthed in Hattusa. A leather jacket over a shirt of scale-armour, however, would have been extremely hot, probably unbearably so on a long route-march in mid-summer.

Almost certainly, Hittite troops on the march clad themselves as lightly as possible. Their campaigns often took them over hundreds of miles, during the hottest part of the year and through desert or semi-desert terrain. The speed with which they could move and the large distances they could cover in a day would have been impossible if they marched in full battle kit. This must have been donned only when they were about to confront the enemy. Perhaps they wore their protective headgear during the march as well as on the field of battle, though in the sculpture of the god on the gate at Hattusa, the helmet may have been included primarily to depict the god in his warrior role.

In the rock sanctuary close to the Hittite capital and now known as Yazılıkaya, 12 gods are depicted in single file, and apparently marching towards the right. They too are wearing short kilts belted at the waist. Their war-like character is indicated by scimitar-like swords, which they clasp in their right hands and carry over their shoulders. We know they are gods because of the cone-like hats that they wear, a sign of divine status. Often thought to represent the 12 gods of the Underworld, they have a clear militaristic aspect. Perhaps they provide a visual illustration of gods actually running before their royal protégés into battle. They wear leather boots with upturned toes. These boots were an essential part of a soldier's issue, worn during the march as well as in battle. Though the warrior-god at Hattusa is barefooted, no Hittite soldier could have survived the rough terrain of Anatolia and the hot sands of the Syrian desert regions without strong, durable footwear.

The 12 gods depicted upon the walls of the Hittite sanctuary at Yazılıkaya. While generally interpreted as Underworld deities, they appear here equipped for battle, and are perhaps marching against the enemy at the head of the Hittite army.

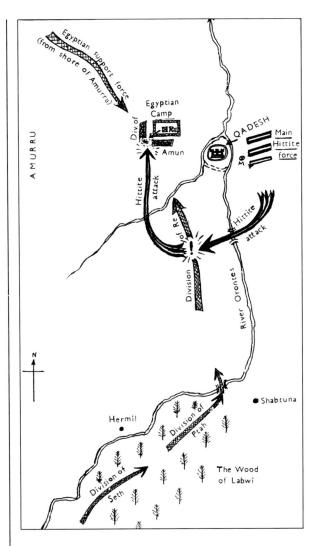

A plan of the Kadesh (also spelt "Qadesh") battle, 1274. From their place of concealment behind the city of Kadesh, the Hittites cross the Orontes river and launch a surprise attack on Ramesses' army, smashing through the Re division and catching the Amun division, which is under Pharaoh's personal command, completely off guard as they set up camp. The timely arrival of Egyptian reinforcements helps save the Egyptians from a complete rout. (From K. Kitchen, *Pharaoh Triumphant*, Warminster, Aris & Phillips, 1982; courtesy Oxbow Books)

We may gain a clearer idea of the dress of Hittite warriors in battle from Egyptian depictions of the battlefield at Kadesh. In contrast to the more lightly clad warrior-god at Hattusa, the soldiers at Kadesh wear neck-to-ankle sleeved garments. The Anatolian scholar James Macqueen has suggested that this garment was tropical kit issued for use in the hot Syrian climate, or a sort of great-coat to be left with the baggage-train when swift action was intended. Perhaps it was a long coat of mail, worn over a cloth garment and donned just before the battle began. The notable absence of shields among the Hittite infantry may support this suggestion, if the garments themselves provided some protection against an enemy's swords and spears.

To judge from both Hittite and Egyptian reliefs, even the highest-ranking Hittite officers seem not to have stood out conspicuously from their troops, as far as battledress and equipment were concerned. From the warrior-god at Hattusa, we probably learn as much about the common soldier's kit while on the march as we do about the kit and accoutrements of the king himself. The differences in weapons and protective equipment between contingents of Hittite troops were probably determined primarily by the roles assigned to them in the battle, and by their places of origin. Thus the armaments of the chariotry differed from those of the infantry. Contingents from different regions may well have worn their own distinctive clothing and armour, and particularly their own distinctive headgear, so that they could easily be identified in the heat and dust of battle. This was of no small importance, given that troops from the same region fought together, under their own commanders.

Weaponry
Shields

The most important item of Hittite defensive equipment was a shield, which probably covered the body from neck to thigh, though Hittite shields are depicted smaller than this in the Kadesh reliefs. They were basically rectangular, with a slightly convex top and bottom and slightly concave sides. Made of leather stretched over a wooden frame, they appear to have been used mainly though not exclusively by the chariot contingent, for which they had the important advantage of being relatively light in comparison with metal shields. Ordinary rectangular shields were used by allied contingents of the Hittites. The smaller round shields that became a feature of Hittite armaments during the neo-Hittite period (1st millennium BC) were apparently not used by the Late Bronze Age Hittites, or at least only in the last decades of their kingdom's existence.

Swords

The standard Hittite weapon used by all ranks and sections of the militia was the short stabbing sword with ribbed blade and crescent-shaped pommel. The blade was sometimes slightly curved, as in the case of the sword or dagger carried by the warrior-god in his belt. While other weapons and military equipment were no doubt stored in the baggage-train during route-marches, the short sword could be conveniently tucked into the soldier's belt, thus ensuring that every member of the Hittite army was at all times armed. Longswords also constituted part of the army's arsenal. In 1991, one such weapon was discovered near the so-called Lion Gate of the Hittite capital. It bears an inscription, which records a victory by the early 14th-century king Tudhaliya over a western coalition of countries commonly known from clay tablet texts as the Assuwan Confederacy. The inscription reads: 'As Tudhaliya the Great King shattered the Assuwan country, he dedicated these swords to the Storm God, his lord.' The sword was perhaps part of the booty of this campaign. Sickle-shaped or slashing swords, like those with which the 12 gods at Yazılıkaya were armed, illustrate another kind of Hittite weapon. In this case the blade was on the outer rather than the inner edge. One advantage of the sickle sword was that it was less prone to snapping than straight-edged swords.

Hittite shield, reconstructed from relief scenes. The leather was stretched tight over a wooden frame. Designed for lightness, and primarily intended to parry blows, it was unlikely to withstand a direct spear thrust or an arrow fired directly at it. (Courtesy Ekip Film)

Stabbing and slashing swords were used for fighting at close quarters, particularly in mountainous terrain or in forested regions where Hittite expeditionary forces were more exposed to surprise attacks by enemy forces. On more open level ground where the Hittite king could deploy his chariotry and use set battle formations, however, the spear, some 2.1–2.4m (7–8ft) in length, was employed to devastating effect by both chariotry and infantry. It served both as a thrusting and a throwing weapon when the order was given to charge an enemy drawn up for battle.

The metal used for all these weapons was bronze – an alloy consisting of about 90 per cent copper and 10 per cent tin, and much tougher than copper on its own. It was long believed that the Hittites owed their success in battle to weapons of iron, supposedly far superior to the bronze weapons used by their contemporaries. This view is wrong. Certainly the Hittites fashioned artefacts out of iron, but this was natural meteoritic iron. Its rarity made it extremely valuable, and items produced from it, including weapons and a throne, were highly prized but intended for ceremonial use, or as special gifts for a king's peers. Apart from its rarity, such iron would have been totally unsuitable for functioning weapons. The technology for smelting the metal had not been developed before the end of the Bronze Age, and neither was the process of mixing carbon with iron to produce steel. Any iron weapons manufactured in this period would have been extremely brittle and far inferior to weapons of bronze.

There was one drawback to the use of bronze. So far, we know of no source in Anatolia where tin was mined in the Late Bronze Age, or at

A horseman with a round shield from Tell Halaf, in north-eastern Syria, dating to the 10th century BC, now in the British Museum. (Courtesy British Museum)

least mined in sufficient quantities to meet the Hittites' needs. This situation meant that they had to import most and probably all of their tin supplies, very likely from sources in Afghanistan via east–west trade routes that passed through Mesopotamia and Syria. It thus became essential to have some control over the regions through which these routes passed.

Bows and arrows

The principal weapon of the Hittite chariot contingent was the bow and arrow. There may also have been contingents of archers in the Hittite infantry, though we have no proof of this. The bow was made of a composite of wood and horn glued together, which gave it much strength and flexibility. The arrow shafts were of wood or reed, and to these bronze arrow heads, often barbed, were attached by a tang. Quivers, probably of leather, held 20 or 30 arrows. Large quantities of these missiles were no doubt manufactured along with other weapons for the Hittite army in government-operated armament factories, and stockpiled in the baggage-train that accompanied the army on the march, ready for rapid distribution to the troops as they prepared for battle. Yet a major conflict could rapidly exhaust the stockpile, and it may have been common practice for supplies to be replenished by subject states in or near the regions where the army was campaigning.

A 10th-century BC relief from the neo-Hittite city of Carchemish on the Euphrates river. The axe is being wielded by the Storm God Teshub. (Courtesy British Museum)

THE HITTITES ON CAMPAIGN

For the Hittites, the thaw of the winter snows would denote the time for the campaigning season to begin. At this time the king would put his troops on alert, for possible mobilization against an enemy who was threatening the security of his realm, or to put down a rebellion amongst his vassal states. Almost inevitably, each new year would bring a fresh crop of crises that could only be resolved by military force. News of such crises would be brought back by the king's messengers from various parts of the kingdom, or sent in reports by the king's loyal vassal rulers in trouble-prone subject territories. These communications indicated the regions where Hittite military intervention might be called for. Conscious of the need to use his military resources in the best way possible, the king had to judge whether a particular crisis required military action, and if so, how large a military expedition was needed to deal with it, and whether he should take personal command of the operation.

Let us suppose that the king has received reports of a major uprising among a number of his subject states, aided and abetted by a foreign power. The crisis is serious enough to warrant a general mobilization of the kingdom's military forces, and significant enough for the king himself to take command. However, he must leave behind a sufficiently strong defence force to ensure that his homeland is protected while the main army is away. This is one of the reasons why he calls up both reservists and civilian soldiers. Some of these will reinforce the ranks of the campaigning army, but others will be used, along with a number of the king's permanent troops, to guard the homeland. The king also sends out a call for military levies from his kingdom's more remote regions. Reinforcements from these regions will ensure that he can maintain his campaigning army at full strength while freeing up significant numbers of his regular and part-time Hittite troops to provide a homeland defence force.

With his bodyguards closely assembled around him, the king prepares to leave his city, at the head of his army. After seeking and gaining the gods' approval for his campaign, he offers up final prayers for a successful outcome in a chapel just inside one of the city's main gates. That done, he acknowledges the salute of the god whose image is carved at the gate's exit, and who will accompany him throughout the campaign. The army leaving the capital with the king is but the core of the army that the king will lead into battle. Along the route, there will be a meeting-place where the entire campaign force, including levies from outlying regions of the kingdoms and perhaps also allied contingents from elsewhere, will assemble. Here the king will inspect a parade of the entire army, and here the troops will reaffirm their oath of allegiance to their sovereign.

Depiction of the last-known Hittite king, Suppiluliuma II, as an archer. He is also armed with a lance. The relief appears, along with a hieroglyphic inscription recording Suppiluliuma's conquests, in the recently discovered 'Südburg' building in Hattusa.

The 'Temple 5' complex in Hattusa, which lies close to the King's Gate. It includes what have tentatively been identified as a palace-annex and three small chapels. The king may have spent his final hours in this precinct, communing with his gods and his ancestors, before setting forth on a military campaign.

The assembly area is also where the king will hold strategy meetings with his chief officers. One or more of these may be members of his own family. He may decide at this point to send a detachment of troops ahead of the main army, in the hope that this mere show of force will suffice to bring the rebels to heel, or that the expeditionary force will put down the rebellion, perhaps by capturing its ringleaders, without the need for committing the entire army to the operation. Or he may send a verbal or written message to the leaders of the rebellion, seeking a diplomatic solution. Hittite kings frequently made every effort to restore order in a rebellious region without military action or with only a minimum use of force, even if they had already led their armies a considerable distance along the campaign trail. Cutting short a campaign already underway meant that the resources so committed could be redeployed to other areas where they were needed. Perhaps more importantly, this decision would enable the manpower to be reassigned at the earliest possible opportunity to the defence of the homeland or, in the case of civilian soldiers, to be returned to their roles as food producers.

As often as not, however, Hittite campaigns had to be fought to the bitter end. It is difficult to overestimate the hardships and challenges that such campaigns regularly entailed, and the logistical problems they involved. Of prime importance was the provisioning of the troops. An army on campaign frequently had to march for hundreds of miles, through arid regions and territories occupied by hostile forces.

Basic rations of flour and bread (called 'soldier-bread') and perhaps also wine were kept in a commissariat, no doubt heavily guarded. The rations were transported in four-wheeled wagons pulled by teams of two oxen or horses, or carried by donkeys in sacks or baskets slung over their backs. These supplies could be replenished en route while the army was still in Hittite subject territory. The soldiers passed through towns where silos had been constructed primarily, it seems, for storing grain and fodder for Hittite troops and their animals while on campaign. Almost 100 Hittite cities are recorded as having these facilities. They are called 'seal-house cities of grain', or 'seal-house cities of fodder'. The enormous grain-storage facilities recently excavated in the Hittite capital, while almost certainly on a much larger scale than any of the provincial 'seal-house' cities, give a good indication of what these storage facilities must have been like, and the highly efficient way in which grain was stored and preserved in them, free of vermin, disease or deterioration through rotting.

Even if sufficient to keep body and soul together, the soldier's food rations were extremely basic, and there must have been considerable temptation for the troops to pillage the towns they passed along or near the campaign route. Such pilfering activities were strictly forbidden, however. No plundering or even foraging was permitted while troops were passing through Hittite subject states. On the other hand, the ruler of such a state could be expected to provide food and drink for a Hittite army en route through his territory, if so requested. This provisioning was covered by strict regulations, and the king guaranteed that anything requisitioned from the local community would be paid for in full. Very likely, provisioning of troops by a local subject kingdom was fairly rare, required only if the army was running low on supplies. Yet once the troops had passed beyond Hittite subject territory, they were free to plunder the lands of their enemies, and perhaps do the same to independent states that had no agreement with their king. They may often have been forced to forage for food in these states as their own rations started to run out.

Granaries at Hattusa. The remains of the built grain pits depicted here were recently discovered on the hill now called Büyükkaya, which lay on Hattusa's north-eastern extremity. Elsewhere in the city, an underground storage complex consisting of two parallel rows of 16 chambers each was brought to light.

Ambush was a constant threat faced by the troops once they had entered enemy or enemy-occupied territory. Almost certainly, reconnaissance parties were regularly sent ahead of the main force both to seek out sources of food and water, and to check for signs of possible surprise enemy attacks. The utmost vigilance was needed. On one occasion, unusual agitation and noise by birds near the route ahead of the Hittite troops betrayed and thwarted an enemy ambush. On another occasion in the early 14th century, in or near a region called Lukka in south-western Turkey, a Hittite expeditionary force was not so fortunate. Its commander was tricked by a treacherous ally into leading his troops into an enemy ambush. The commander was killed and his force annihilated.

A Hittite commander made every effort to draw an enemy into open battle – by burning the enemy's crops and villages, for example. If he succeeded, then his forces were almost invariably victorious. Wherever the Hittites fought in the Near Eastern world, their battlefield training, and the skills of their charioteers in particular, almost always guaranteed their success – provided the enemy met them on open ground. However, an enemy that resorted to ambush, to sudden attacks and withdrawals and to forcing the Hittites to come after them in mountainous or thickly forested terrain where chariotry was useless, could prove a formidable, elusive and sometimes unconquerable opponent. Also, an enemy who sought protection behind the walls of a heavily fortified city sometimes forced the Hittites into a long and costly siege, where the besiegers could end up suffering as much, if not more than, the besieged. A Hittite king often did all he could to avoid laying siege to a well-defended city, or indeed taking any city by force. The enemy was always given the option of voluntary submission. Should their ruler reject this option, and his city or kingdom was taken by force, then by right of conquest the city or kingdom was plundered of everything of value, and torched. Its inhabitants and its livestock became spoils of war.

When a campaign had ended, the troops were then faced with what was often the most physically taxing and most dangerous part of the

Ambush. This reconstruction reflects a notorious episode in the early 14th century BC when the treacherous Hittite vassal Madduwatta joined the enemy for an ambush on a Hittite expeditionary force, killing its commander Kisnapili. (Courtesy Ekip Film)

Postern gate. Postern tunnels were a typical feature of Bronze Age fortifications. They provided the defenders of a city with access to and exit from it during a siege, either for gathering provisions, or for making surprise attacks upon the enemy. The external gate to the postern in the south wall of Hattusa is shown here.

entire enterprise – the march back home. If a campaign had begun late in the campaigning season or been unexpectedly prolonged, the pressure on the commander was all the greater to get the army and its spoils back to the homeland before the winter snows set in. Occasionally, when a campaign had not been completed by the end of the season, the troops were obliged to spend winter away from home – in a temporary encampment established in alien and sometimes hostile territory, probably in very harsh conditions, with meagre rations. Opportunities for foraging in mid-winter were obviously extremely limited. This was all the more reason to ensure the successful completion of a campaign within a single season, and in time to return to the homeland.

Victory itself also imposed greatly increased liabilities on the homeward-bound troops. The safe transport back to Hatti of the booty that came from military successes was in itself an enterprise of major proportions. Carts stacked with the glittering trophies of conquest, including the images wrought in precious metals of the vanquished cities' gods, life-size bulls of gold, chariots of silver and boats with silver-plated prows, must have substantially slowed each day's progress. But in many campaigns, by far the greatest part of the spoils consisted of human booty and livestock. Hittite military records refer repeatedly to the transportation of people, sheep and cattle from the conquered territories back to the homeland. The number of transportees ran sometimes to the hundreds, sometimes to the thousands; sometimes the prisoners and captured livestock were too numerous to count. 'The transportees I brought to the palace numbered 15,000,' reports the Hittite king Mursili II in the aftermath of one of his victories. 'However, the transportees, the cattle and the sheep which the generals, the infantry, and the chariotry of Hattusa brought back were beyond count.' At the end of a campaign, the king may have returned to Hattusa as quickly as possible with as many of his troops as he could afford to take with him. However, the supervision, provisioning and protection of thousands of prisoners and livestock on the march undoubtedly meant the commitment of a large part of the army to ensuring that they eventually reached their destination.

Let us try to imagine the situation. The Hittite army, already wearied by the demands of months of active campaigning far from their homeland, now had the responsibility of feeding and guarding on a trek of perhaps several hundred miles large numbers of unwilling transportees and even larger numbers of livestock. Adequate supplies of food had to be found for all of these to ensure that they remained fit enough to survive the journey. This burden must have considerably slowed the army's progress and increased its vulnerability to enemy attack. Bands of brigands were ready to exploit any slackening of vigilance to plunder the baggage train, rustle livestock that had strayed from the herd, then escape with their prizes to their mountain hideouts. The booty-people needed strict, constant supervision to ensure they made no attempt to escape.

The Hittites' transportation system caused much human tragedy for its victims. Men, women and children all became part of the spoils of war. Families were torn apart, husbands and wives, children and parents were separated, proud warriors were reduced to slavery. All down to the smallest child were forced to undergo the rigours of walking hundreds of miles, often in extremely harsh conditions. Casualties along the way are likely to have been high. For those who survived the ordeal, the prospect at the end of it was lifelong servitude in the land of the conqueror. Very likely there were frequent escape attempts, and no doubt recaptured escapees were severely punished in an attempt to discourage future attempts. One way in which the Hittites sought to minimize such attempts was to close off to the prisoners places to which they might escape. Local rulers whose countries might serve as possible places of refuge were strictly warned against providing shelter to escaped Hittite prisoners. Failure to heed this warning could result in severe reprisals.

From recently discovered letters in a provincial centre of the Hittite homeland, another disturbing possibility has emerged concerning the treatment of prisoners-of-war by Hittite warriors. References are made to transportees who had apparently been settled in the frontier regions of the Hittite kingdom, close to their own homeland. A significant number of them appear to have been blind. It is a distinct possibility that they had their eyes put out to prevent their trying to escape back home, or as a warning to others of the consequences of escape attempts. Blind or blinded prisoners could still be gainfully employed. One of the letters indicates that they were used as labour gangs in the local mill-houses, where they were presumably shackled to the poles that turned the mill wheels.[4]

In spite of the many problems and dangers that transporting thousands of booty-people and livestock must have entailed, the regularity of the practice indicates that the benefits that the conquerors gained from it outweighed the costs and the risks. On the one hand, the culling of a rebellious state's most able-bodied men would have significantly reduced that state's ability to rebel again, at least in the short term. On the other hand, transportation was an important means of restocking both the military and the agricultural personnel of the homeland – an important consideration, given the substantial drain on Hittite manpower caused by the annual military campaigns.

---

4. See H.A. Hoffner, 'The Treatment and Long-Term Use of Persons Captured in Battle according to Masat Texts', in K. A. Yener and H. A. Hoffner (eds), *Recent Developments in Hittite Archaeology and History, Papers in Memory of Hans G. Güterbock* (Winona Lake, 2002), pp.61–72. Also see T. R. Bryce, *Letters of the Great Kings of the Ancient Near East* (London, 2003), pp.173–74.

Hittite chariot, reconstructed. Chariots had to be light enough to ensure speed and manoeuvrability in battle, but also sufficiently robust to carry three warriors, and endure the rigours of a long campaigning season.

TRAINING AND DISCIPLINE

Training and discipline contributed hugely to the string of victories won by the Hittites on the battlefield. Unfortunately, we have little information about Hittite military training programmes. Without doubt, the most highly trained troops were those of the professional army, and very likely the reservists were also required to report for training on a regular basis. The elite chariot contingent probably underwent the most rigorous training programme, under the supervision of specially appointed training officers. A fragmentary early Hittite text provides a few pieces of information about this programme.[5] Developing a high level of competence in bowmanship was an important part of it, perhaps the most important part. The bow was the chariot fighter's main weapon, and skill in using it needed to be of a very high order, since the charioteer had to fit his arrow and fire it accurately from a rapidly moving chariot, which must often have swerved and bumped over rough ground. From what we can glean from our fragmentary text, training in bowmanship went well beyond simply learning how to discharge an arrow. It also included instruction in sharpening arrow-heads, the aerodynamics of an arrow's flight and the correct way to hold the bow and use it effectively under the most adverse conditions. Probably at the end of their training programme, the bowmen-charioteers were obliged to demonstrate their proficiency before the king. Those who hit a specified target received a cup of wine. Those who missed were forced to drink something much nastier (we cannot be sure precisely what, though urine-drinking was a known form of punishment in the Hittite world), and were further humiliated by being forced to run naked before their comrades.

Night manoeuvres also formed part of the charioteer's training programme. As we shall see, such manoeuvres played an important role in Hittite military strategy. Given the potential hazards of night operations for rapidly moving vehicles, intensive night training was essential for both charioteers and their horses.

---

5. See R. H. Beal, *The Organization of the Hittite Military* (Heidelberg, 1992), pp.127–29.

A detailed manual has survived concerning the preparation of Hittite horses for chariot combat. It is credited to a man called Kikkuli, one of the Hittites' Mitannian prisoners-of-war. The training regime for the chariot horses extended over a period of 214 days, with 32 of these days devoted to night manoeuvres. Night training was intended to familiarize the animals with battle conditions under cover of darkness. Also, much of the travel done by the Hittite army may have taken place at night, to avoid unnecessary exposure to the heat of the day. The manual contains many technical terms whose meanings are uncertain, but it is clear that much of the training programme addressed aspects such as the horse's speed, strength, promptness to obey commands and, above all, stamina. There was a severe culling of animals before the programme began. Only the fittest and strongest animals survived the cull. Indeed, the horses were bred as much for endurance and stamina as for speed and manoeuvrability in battle. Like their drivers, the horses often had to travel hundreds of miles to the battlefield, and still be able to operate at their peak in the battle itself.

At all levels in the military hierarchy, Hittite soldiers were no doubt trained to a high level of physical fitness to ensure that even after a long, gruelling march they were still in a state of battle preparedness, ready to take on an enemy who was fresh and had simply awaited their adversary's arrival. Above all, Hittite troops were trained to accept and act upon without question the commands of their superior officers, and never to break ranks or retreat even in the face of apparently insurmountable odds. Strict discipline must have helped ensure that these requirements were met. Discipline and punishment at all levels were almost certainly harsh, though we have little specific information. Desertion was a serious crime, and instances of it were referred directly to the king, very likely an indication that it was a capital offence. Troops were also expected to report instances of disloyal acts by their own officers, and vice versa. Failure to do so rendered the non-complying person liable to the death penalty alongside the offender.

Death or mutilation by blinding were punishments with which a king threatened his officers who did not respond promptly to his commands:

> Say to Kassu and Zilapiya: 'As soon as this letter reaches you, come with all haste before His Majesty. If not, [my men] will come to you and blind you on the spot!'

> You Pipappa, bring the UKU.UŠ troops [i.e. professional standing army troops] across as quickly as possible. Bring them here to the army. If you do not, you will come [and] you will die![6]

These orders and threats were issued by King Tudhaliya III at a time when the kingdom was facing one of the gravest crises in its history. The slightest dereliction of duty could not be tolerated, but the threatened punishments of death and mutilation may have been uncharacteristically harsh. Nevertheless, we know of other cases where negligence or incompetence in the king's service was punishable by death, and it could well be that dereliction of duty in the king's army was regularly punished in this way.

6. Extracts from letters in the Masat archive, trans. Bryce, *Letters*, p.180.

Military service took on a variety of forms, and encompassed a wide range of duties and skills. Fulfilment of these duties required different kinds of training, much of which probably took place on the job, under the supervision of the soldiers' immediate superiors.

BELIEF AND BELONGING

We have noted that the core of the Hittite defence forces was a professional standing army, which was employed by the state all year round. They were the kingdom's elite fighting force, and no doubt took much pride in their status. Many of them may have been handpicked by the king himself, especially at officer level. Undoubtedly, they built up a strong sense of identity, and strong bonds of loyalty within their own ranks. The first loyalty of each of them, however, was to his king, his commander-in-chief. Indeed it was to the king rather than to the state that he gave his allegiance. The standing army, therefore, was the core military body that gave coherence to the kingdom's entire fighting force.

From within the ranks of the standing army, there came the most elite group of all – the king's personal bodyguards. There were two groups of royal bodyguards. The more prestigious of them was called the *MESHEDI*. They were armed with spears and stationed on 24-hour guard duty, in shifts of 12 at a time, in the palace's main courtyard. They were the king's first line of protection. Very likely, they wore a distinctive uniform. They formed a close inner ring around the king whenever he went forth into and from his capital to take part in religious festivals, to make pilgrimages to the

Entrance to the acropolis, Hattusa. The gate-building that was constructed here provided official access to the palace from a viaduct leading from the south. It would have been guarded 24 hours a day by members of the king's elite bodyguard. Guard-rooms flanked the gate-building's entrance.

various holy cities of his realm and to lead military campaigns. They were among the most trusted of all the king's subjects. A second group of bodyguards, also 12 in number at any one time, were known as the 'Men of the Golden Spear'. The principal duty of both groups was to keep the king safe from harm at all times. More than any other troops, they gave their loyalty to the king alone. No doubt a rigorous selection process helped ensure that they were above suspicion, and had all the qualities necessary to fulfil the requirements of their office.

The unconditional loyalty that all troops were expected to give to the king and his family is emphasized in an oath-taking ceremony that marked the induction of the lower order of officers and the rank-and-file troops into the army:

> They bring the garments of a woman, a distaff and a mirror, they break an arrow and you speak as follows: 'Is not this that you see here garments of a woman? We have them here for [the ceremony of taking] the oath. Whoever breaks these oaths and does evil to the king and the queen and the princes, let these oaths change him from a man into a woman! Let them change his troops into women, let them dress them in the fashion of women and cover their heads with a length of cloth! Let them break the bows, arrows, and clubs in their hands and let them put in their hands distaff and mirror!'[7]

The importance of having a core militia whose allegiance was focused on the person of the king becomes all the clearer when we consider the nature of the rest of the Hittite fighting forces, and more generally the nature of the rest of the kingdom. Hittite armies were cobbled together for specific military operations, their composition varying according to the nature and extent of the campaign being fought, and the regions where it was fought. Much of the campaign force may have consisted of levies drawn from a wide range of peripheral areas of the kingdom. That is to say, a substantial portion of a Hittite army was often made up of troops who had very little if any sense of allegiance to the king or the kingdom on whose behalf they were fighting. They were there simply because a local ruler had signed a compact with his Hittite overlord to provide troops for the Hittite army when called upon to do so; in a few cases they were there because they had hired out their services to the king. As we shall see, battles were largely won by the king's standing militia, especially the chariotry, with the great majority of the rank-and-file troops gathered from other regions acting merely in an ancillary role. These troops could have had little sense of personal commitment to the kingdom of Hatti, which in many cases had imposed its rule by force upon them. This situation made it essential for groups from the various regions to be barracked together and fight together during military campaigns, under their own leaders. It was their bonding with each other and with their local commander, rather than any sense of allegiance to Hatti, that underpinned their contribution to Hittite military successes.

---

7. Extract from Soldiers' Oath, trans. by A. Goetze in J. B. Pritchard (ed.), *Ancient Near Eastern Texts relating to the Old Testament*, 3rd edn (Princeton, 1969), p.354.

There were no doubt a number of times during a campaign when morale amongst the troops dropped to a low level, whether due to the physical demands imposed on them by harsh environmental conditions, or through shortages of rations, disease, harassment by enemy guerrilla bands or a military setback. No doubt the king and his officers were fully aware of possible morale problems and had various ways of dealing with them. Special rituals seem to have played a role in boosting morale when the soldiers' spirits were flagging. One of the rituals reads thus:

> When it gets scary in the field for a 'lord of the army' or when all goes right for the enemy in battle and it doesn't go right for our young men, one performs the following ritual: Throw hot fir cones and hot stones into water. As the fir cones and the stones hiss and then get cold and become silent, so may the manhood, battle, and awareness of you [the enemy] and your troops likewise grow cold and be extinguished. Like a stone, let them become dumb and silent… The gods march on our side. The gods have given to our army young men with manhood and bravery.[8]

Rituals such as these had a very powerful effect on many aspects of life in the Hittite world. Belief in their potency went a long way towards ensuring the soldiers' success.

THE ARMY IN BATTLE

Chariotry

Chariotry provided the elite corps of the Hittite army. It was primarily on their performance that the Hittites' successes in open battle depended. The chariot had been introduced into Anatolia by the early 16th century BC, probably from the Hurrian world. It was a very light vehicle, consisting of a wooden frame with leather covering. The car was mounted on a wide

---

8. Translated by Beal, 'Hittite Military Organization', p.552.

axle with six-spoked wooden wheels. To begin with, it was similar to the chariot used in Egypt. It was pulled by two stallions attached to either side of a long pole that extended from the underside of the car. Initially the Hittite chariot, like its Egyptian counterpart, contained two men – the driver and the fighter. By the time of the battle of Kadesh, however, the Hittites had introduced a third man into the chariot. This man carried a shield that he used to protect both the driver and the fighter. The fighter could thus concentrate on attacking the enemy, and the driver on manoeuvring the vehicle and keeping it upright, while the defender fended off missiles and spear thrusts aimed at his comrades.

The fighter was armed with both spear and bow and arrow. The spear may have been used primarily in the initial battle charge, for hurling or thrusting at the enemy. After discharging this weapon, the fighter may then have used his bow and arrow, extracting the bow from a case attached to the side of his chariot, and his arrows from a quiver slung over his back. In the hands of a skilled chariot fighter, the bow and arrow could be used with devastating effect against an enemy's infantry ranks, but ultimate victory probably depended very largely on the outcome of contests between opposing chariot forces. Many of the enemies that the Hittites encountered could put chariots into the field, often in considerable numbers. King Hattusili III informs us that when he governed the northern part of the Hittite kingdom during his brother's reign, one of the rulers in the region brought no fewer than 800 chariots into battle against him. This is probably an exaggeration, but there is no doubt that the military forces of even relatively small kingdoms included some hundreds of chariots.

Rigorous training must have given Hittite charioteers the edge over many of the enemy contingents. But they were far from invincible, particularly when confronting the army of another great king whose charioteers were equally well trained and equipped. Ramesses' father Seti I boasted of inflicting a resounding defeat on the Hittite king Muwattalli at Kadesh some ten years or so before Muwattalli's encounter there with his son. Victory in this first showdown at Kadesh may well have been due to the superior performance of the Egyptian chariotry. The defeat may have prompted the development of the Hittite three-man chariot that was to shatter Ramesses' first division at Kadesh in 1274. But chariots carrying three warriors had their disadvantages. They must have been slower and less manoeuvrable than the standard two-man chariot. The chariot's wheels were mounted under the middle of the chariot car rather than under its rear to bear the extra weight. This configuration would have made the chariot less stable, and more likely to topple over when driven at speed or when making a tight turn. Disadvantages like these, however, were probably more than compensated for by the fact that the chariot fighter could focus entirely on shooting down or spearing the enemy, relying on his shield-bearing comrade beside him to protect him from the enemy's weapons.

On open plains, battles were won and lost by the chariot contingents, with the infantry playing no more than a subordinate, backup role. Such is borne out in Egyptian scenes of the battle of Kadesh, where the infantry appear not in the role of active fighters but as defenders of the army's equipment and baggage, and as protectors of their commander-in-chief. But on rough, uneven ground, and in mountainous terrain, the

A: Hittite warriors

B: Recruiting scene

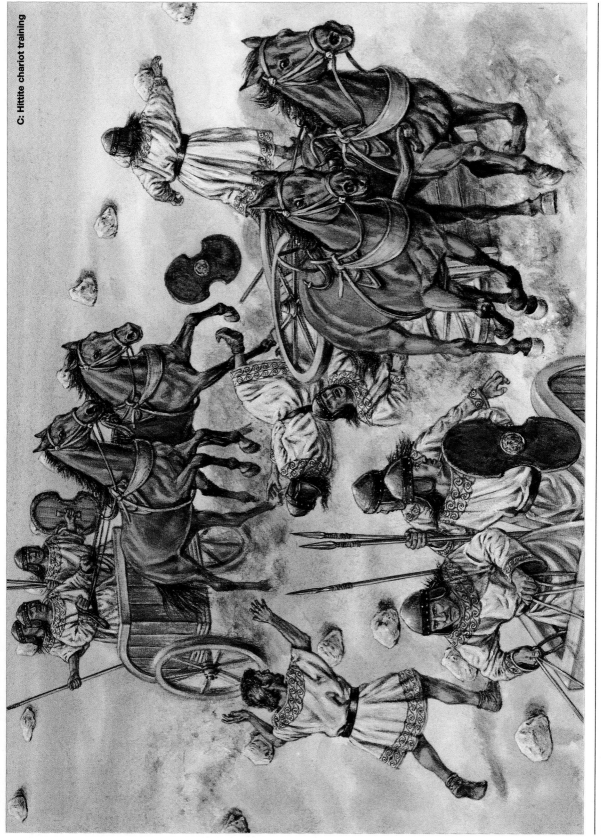

C: Hittite chariot training

C

D: Hittite night attack on enemy city

D

E: Kings harnessed to a baggage wagon

G: The battle of Kadesh

G

infantry assumed a much more active role – in storming mountain or forest refuges, engaging the enemy in combat on a one-to-one basis, running to ground their leaders, capturing and escorting prisoners, and plundering and torching enemy or rebel towns and communities. King Mursili II tells us of the storming of a mountain stronghold that was inaccessible to horses:

> I, My Sun, went to Mount Arinnanda. This mountain is very steep and extends out into the sea. It is also very high, difficult of access, and rocky, and it is impossible for horses to advance up it. The transportees held it en masse and the infantry were above en masse. Since it was impossible for horses to advance up the mountain, I, My Sun, went before the army on foot and went up Mount Arinnanda on foot.[9]

Chariots were sometimes used for transporting the king from one place to another in religious festivals, and very likely the king travelled by chariot on his spiritual pilgrimages throughout his realm. Other high-ranking officials may also have used chariots for transportation. It seems inconceivable, however, that war chariots were actually driven by the charioteers from a military expedition's starting-point to the battlefield. War chariots were not robust structures, for they were built essentially for speed and manoeuvrability in battle. They would have been totally unfit for this purpose if driven hundreds of miles prior to

Hittite three-man chariot. This comes from an Egyptian relief scene of the battle of Kadesh, commissioned by Ramesses II. The depiction of Hittite chariots with rear-mounted wheels is probably a mistake on the part of the Egyptian sculptures. The wheels were almost certainly attached under the middle of the carriage.

---

9. Extract from *Annals of Mursili II* [Die Annalen des Mursilis].

Reconstructed baggage cart, used for carrying food and military supplies (the latter no doubt including spare parts for chariots and large reserves of arrows and spears) along the campaign route. Once loaded up, the sides and top of the cart would presumably have been covered in animal skins or other materials stitched together.

Oxen at Kadesh. An Egyptian depiction, from the Kadesh reliefs, of animals used to pull the baggage carts, and no doubt when necessary to provide meat on the hoof.

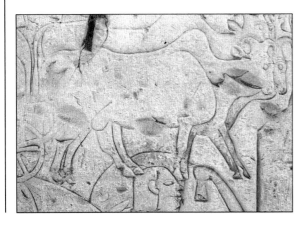

battle over frequently rough terrain, even assuming they managed to survive the journey in one piece. We must also spare a thought for the horses who pulled them in battle. Even the fittest and strongest of these animals would have had their battle-preparedness seriously impaired had they been used as transport animals, hauling manned chariots for perhaps weeks on end before conflict began. As we have noted, Hittite armies on campaign were accompanied by large baggage-trains; supplies and small items of equipment were carried by donkeys, larger items by four-wheeled ox-drawn carts. These larger items must have included the chariots. Even so, chariots may well have required regular repairs and maintenance throughout a campaigning season. Presumably, large numbers of spare parts were also taken on the campaign to replace irreparable breakages or to avoid the need for lengthy repair jobs, for which there might be little or no time.

Horse riders armed with bows and arrows are known throughout the Late Bronze Age Near Eastern, Egyptian and Mycenaean worlds. Their numbers appear to have been small, but they clearly belonged to a military context, and it is tempting to think of them as forming small cavalry units. Yet we have neither written nor visual evidence to indicate that cavalry played an active role in battle in this period. More likely, horse riders served in the army as scouts and messengers rather than as part of a fighting force. They carried out reconnaissance missions, conveyed messages between unit leaders and their commanding officers, and carried dispatches from the battlefield back to the base of operations or to the royal capital. They were armed purely for their own defence while performing communication duties.

Siege warfare

Laying siege to a well-defended city was often a costly operation, since it could tie up for long periods troops who might be urgently required for service in other parts of the kingdom. Before beginning the siege of a city, a Hittite commanding officer would call upon the city's ruler to surrender and throw his gates open; if he did so, his city would be spared the plunder and destruction that would inevitably follow its capture by force. In most cases, the Hittites far preferred the peaceful surrender of a city than the implementation of a siege. Thus King Mursili II, after marching right up to the walls of a treacherous vassal's capital with the object of razing it to the ground, changed his mind at the very last minute when the vassal's aged mother came out of the city and threw herself at his knees. She begged the king to show mercy to her son and spare his city. Mursili agreed, and the city was spared, on the understanding that its ruler would henceforth be a loyal and obedient subject. He was moved, he said, by feelings of compassion

towards an old woman pleading for her son. In actual fact, the king's decision not to attack was based on much sounder, more pragmatic reasons. The campaigning season was drawing rapidly to an end, and the troops had a long march ahead of them to reach their homeland. The last thing they could have wanted was a protracted siege that would almost certainly mean wintering in the field, with food supplies running short and with limited opportunities for replenishing these supplies as winter deepened. Instead of admitting this fact, Mursili preferred to highlight his decision as an act of Hittite compassion and mercy shown to a disloyal, treacherous vassal, who little deserved such consideration but was now ready to admit the error of his ways.

There were, however, occasions when Hittite armies had no alternative but to lay siege to a city. Here the infantry came into its own. Attempts would be made to force entry into the city by breaching its walls or wooden gates with a battering ram, or by setting fire to the gates. Night attacks were sometimes launched in an attempt to catch the defenders by surprise, or to cause confusion among them. But even if the defences were breached in this manner, the fiercest fighting might be yet to come. We hear of a city called Hassuwa that courageously held out against its Hittite attackers. Three times its citizens rallied their forces against the Hittites before the city finally fell. There was no reward for their courage. They had resisted the demand to surrender, and now suffered the consequences. Hassuwa was thoroughly plundered and torched, and its king suffered the abject humiliation of being harnessed, along with another defeated local ruler, to one of the baggage carts used for conveying the spoils taken from his people back to the Hittite capital.

If the fortifications of a city could not be breached, and the defenders prevented the attackers from bursting through the city's main gates, the infantry were set to work on various other means of forcing entry – digging tunnels under the walls, building earth ramps up the walls, or emplacing siege towers that provided access to the city across the top of the walls. The besiegers had to be on constant alert against sallies from the defenders, and fierce battles between besiegers and besieged were sometimes fought at the gates themselves. A substantial number of Hittite troops had to be deployed to block all entrances to and exits from the city, in an attempt to cut it off from communication with its allies, and from access to outside sources of food. The attackers also needed constant access to food supplies. Detachments of the besieging force often had to go on foraging expeditions, in themselves dangerous operations where they risked enemy attack and ambush. On many an occasion, the besieging army may have suffered from food shortages almost as much as the besieged.

The most famous description of a Hittite siege comes from a literary text that describes a Hittite investment of the northern Syrian city called Urshu. The value of this text as a historical source of information has been much debated by scholars. It does, however, give us useful information about the nature of a Hittite siege, and the difficulties the Hittites sometimes had in achieving success in a military operation of this kind against a determined enemy. Urshu apparently held out for six months, and the Hittite king soundly rebuked his officers for their incompetence and timidity:

> They broke the battering-ram. The king was angry and his face was grim: 'They constantly bring me bad news; may the Storm God carry you away in a flood!... Be not idle! Make a battering-ram in the Hurrian manner and let it be brought into place. Hew a great battering-ram from the mountains of Hassu and let it be brought into place. Begin to heap up earth. When you have finished, let every one take post. Only let the enemy give battle, then his plans will be confounded.' ... [Subsequently the king rebukes his general Santas for the inordinate delay in doing battle.] 'Why have you not given battle? You stand on chariots of water, you are almost turned into water yourself... You had only to kneel before him and you would have killed him or at least frightened him. But as it is you have behaved like a woman!'[10]

Naval warfare

The homeland of the kingdom of Hatti was landlocked, and had not even one navigable river. Nevertheless, there were times when it claimed control over the island of Cyprus, the land called Alasiya in Hittite texts. Nominal though this control may have been, it does imply that the Hittites had the means of getting to the island. Alasiya was never a great power in its own right, but its strategic location in the eastern Mediterranean made Hittite access to it important, particularly in the 13th century when the kingdom of Hatti became increasingly dependent on grain imports, which required sea transport from Egypt and the Levantine states. Ships must have been supplied by one of the kingdom's coastal vassal states, most likely the kingdom of Ugarit on the Levantine coast. Until almost the end of the Hittite kingdom, the ships were probably used largely as commercial vessels and military transports. An inscription from the reign of one of the last kings, Tudhaliya IV, commemorates a Hittite conquest of Alasiya, almost certainly carried out by a Hittite force of marines:

10. Extract from Siege of Urshu text, trans. O. R. Gurney, *The Hittites* (London, 1990), pp.148–49.

'I seized the king of Alasiya with his wives, his children... All the goods, including silver and gold, and all the captured people I removed and brought home to Hattusa. I enslaved the country of Alasiya, and made it tributary on the spot.' Then, in the reign of the last Hittite king Suppiluliuma II, we hear for the first time of Hittite naval operations conducted by the Hittites off the coast of Alasiya: 'I, Suppiluliuma, the Great King, immediately [crossed/reached?] the sea. The ships of Alasiya met me in the sea three times for battle, and I smote them; and I seized

the ships and set fire to them in the sea. But when I arrived on dry land, the enemies from Alasiya came in multitude against me for battle.'[11]

These three naval engagements are ominous indicators of the crises engulfing the Hittite world in the kingdom's final years. During the last decades of the 13th and the early decades of the 12th centuries BC, the land of Hatti seems to have become increasingly dependent on grain imports from Egypt and the crop-producing farmlands of the vassal states along the Levantine coast. Prolonged droughts in the homeland regions and shortages in agricultural labour may have contributed to this dependence. Grain shipments were brought by sea from the Egyptian Delta and from ports in the Levant. The grain was unloaded at a port called Ura on the southern Anatolian coast, and then transported overland to the Hittite kingdom. But the grain vessels were vulnerable to attack by both privateers and ships in the employ of a power hostile to Hatti. Alasiya seems to have been used as a base for launching these attacks. It was vital that the grain routes be protected, and for this reason Hatti assumed the role of a naval power in the last years of its existence. The Hittites clearly had to rely on their coastal states to provide both the necessary shipping to defend the grain routes, and no doubt also the captains and crews with the experience and the ability to outmanoeuvre and destroy an enemy fleet on the open sea. But the military operations were conducted on land as well as by sea. Very likely the Hittite navy's

11. Translations after H. G. Güterbock, 'The Hittite Conquest of Cyprus Reconsidered', *Journal of Near Eastern Studies*, 26 (1967), pp.77–78.

fighting force included a large number of Hittite troops who took on the enemy's land forces after the Hittite navy had destroyed their ships at sea.

The size of Bronze Age fleets was small. A text from Ugarit records that a mere seven enemy vessels were sufficient to wreak havoc upon the cities along the eastern Mediterranean coast. Ammurapi, king of Ugarit, sought assistance from the Hittite viceroy stationed at Carchemish on the Euphrates river. But his appeal met with a less than enthusiastic response. Ammurapi was told that he must use his own resources to protect his capital as best he could against the enemy:

> As for what you have written to me: 'Ships of the enemy have been seen at sea!' Well, you must remain firm. Indeed for your part, where are your troops, your chariots stationed? Are they not stationed near you? No? Behind the enemy, who press upon you? Surround your towns with ramparts. Have your troops and chariots enter there, and await the enemy with great resolution![12]

The crisis confronting the Ugaritic king became even more desperate when news came that his own ships and crews were actually collaborating with the approaching enemy they had been sent out to repel.

Piracy and other naval operations were not confined to the high seas. Seaborne raiders often attacked cities along the coastlands of southern Anatolia, Syria-Palestine, Egypt and Cyprus. Indeed in the 14th century a king of Alasiya wrote indignantly to the pharaoh Akhenaten, when the latter accused the Alasiyan people of aiding and abetting the enterprises of pirates who had been raiding his coastal cities. The Alasiyan king hotly rejected the accusation, declaring that his country too was a victim of raids by pirates from the Lukka lands in southern Anatolia: 'Why does my brother speak in these terms to me? "Does not my brother know what is going on?" As far as I am concerned, I have done nothing of the sort! Indeed each year the Lukka people seize towns in my own land!'[13]

The best-known of all seaborne attacks in the Late Bronze Age is the onslaught by the so-called Sea Peoples upon Egypt's Delta during the reign of the pharaoh Ramesses III (c.1184–1153). Ramesses depicted their attack, in both word and picture, as part of a massive land and sea movement by large groups of marauders, who destroyed many of the great centres of Bronze Age civilization in their progress, including the kingdom of Hatti. Though the historical reliability of Ramesses' version of events is open to question, the Sea Peoples' invasion of Egypt almost certainly represents the culmination of many decades, perhaps centuries, of attacks launched by sea raiders against other ships at sea, as well as against cities located along the eastern Mediterranean coastlands.

THE LIFE AND DUTIES OF A SOLDIER

A Hittite soldier's duties were many and varied. They went well beyond the basic tasks of going on campaign and fighting the enemy. Charioteers may well have devoted a large part of their time, when they were not on campaign, to the selection of young stallions for training, and the training

---

12. Trans. J. Nougayrol et al., *Ugaritica V, Mission de Ras Shamra Tome XVI* (Paris, 1968), pp.85–86, No.23.
13. *Amarna letters*, 38, lines 7–12.

process itself. Foot-soldiers performed a variety of other duties. We have noted that the king's two groups of bodyguards, the *MESHEDI* and the 'Men of the Golden Spear', had the principal task of guarding the king's person in the course of whatever activities he was engaged upon. A great deal of their time was probably spent on basic sentry duty outside the king's quarters, whether in the palace in Hattusa, in royal residences dispersed throughout regional centres of the kingdom or on campaign. Individuals among them could also be called upon to act as messengers sent on special missions. The bodyguards had a role to play in the religious festivals in which the king took part, not only as guards but as performers in particular rituals. They also participated in contests associated with the festivals. We hear of a footrace in which the *MESHEDI* competed, the prize for the winner apparently being the privilege of holding the reins of the king's horse while the king dismounted. Occasionally, one of the bodyguards might be called upon to act as royal executioner. We learn of an instance in which a golden spearman was instructed to harness together, like cattle, a governor guilty of embezzling funds and the man sent to replace him. While they were in this state, the golden spearman was ordered to execute one of the guilty man's relatives, ensuring that his blood spattered the garments of both the former and present governor. He then brought both men before the king, so that the king could see for himself the blood of the executed man on their garments.

Escort duty was one of the regular services provided by contingents of troops, probably from the standing army. The need for such a service arose when the king of Hatti sent a diplomatic mission to a fellow Great King. Those sent on such missions included the king's highest diplomatic representatives, sometimes members of his own family, along with a retinue of scribes and other officials. Most importantly, the mission was accompanied by a consignment of valuable gifts for the king's 'royal brother'. Many hundreds of beautifully wrought objects, often of precious and semi-precious materials, made up this consignment, as we know from the detailed lists of them that often accompanied the letters from one king to another. The gift consignments offered a highly attractive target to the brigands who infested many of the regions through which the diplomatic cortège had to pass. A strong military escort, made up of both infantry and chariotry, was essential to ensure safe passage for the mission's personnel and the precious cargo entrusted to them.

A strong escort was also needed when Near Eastern kings sent their daughters to become the brides of their royal brothers. These were occasions for an even more lavish consignment of gifts, to be bestowed upon the bridegroom at the journey's end. King Hattusili III sent two of his daughters to Egypt (some years apart) to become brides of Ramesses II. From the letters that passed between Ramesses and Hattusili's wife Puduhepa, we have fairly detailed information about the arrangements for the progress and security of the wedding party on the journey to Egypt. A substantial military force was needed to protect it, because of its highly distinguished personnel, and the costly gifts that accompanied them. What further necessitated a large escort was the inclusion among the wedding presents of considerable numbers of cattle and sheep, along with prisoners taken by the Hittites from the Kaskan tribes. The Kaskan people were noted for their ferocity, and Ramesses urged Puduhepa to make sure that they were adequately guarded, to prevent their escaping and menacing other travellers in the region. There is little doubt that the escort for the wedding party assumed the proportions of a small army. The fact that its commander was the Hittite king's eldest son Nerikkaili indicates both its size and the importance of the responsibility with which it was entrusted.

Almost certainly, standing troops were employed on public works projects, including bridge-building, the construction of royal residences for the king and above all the fortification and refortification of Hittite cities. Other standing troops were stationed in newly annexed territories or potentially unstable parts of the kingdom as a kind of police force, with instructions to keep the peace in the region, suppress any local uprisings and engage in surveillance activities on the king's behalf.

Frontier defences

Undoubtedly one of the most important tasks of the Hittite militia when not on campaign was the defence of the frontier regions of the kingdoms. Wherever possible, the Hittites preferred to leave the maintenance of order in the subject territories to the local vassal rulers. This policy was partly a matter of diplomacy to avoid the provocation that a permanent Hittite military presence in a vassal state might arouse. By and large, the vassal states were free of Hittite interference, provided their local ruler toed the Hittite line. But more importantly, the ongoing need for the Hittites to use their military resources as economically as possible meant that only those areas seen to be particularly vulnerable to enemy attack were defended by Hittite garrisons. Such areas were, particularly, precarious frontier territories, like the Hittite buffer zones called the Upper and Lower Lands, which lay near the peripheral regions of the homeland, and the border zone in Syria between Hittite and Egyptian subject territory.

Map showing the locations of three frontier towns (Sapinuwa, Tapikka and Sarissa) on the Hittite homeland's northern and eastern peripheries. Tablet archives discovered in these towns shed valuable light on the dangers often faced by the populations living in these regions.

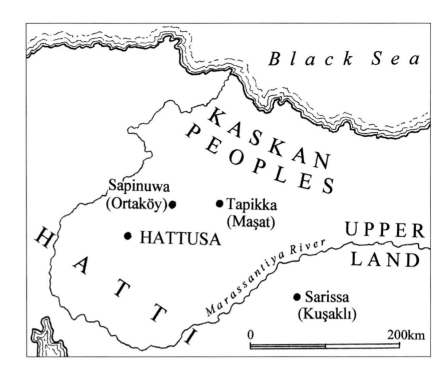

For this last region, we have a vivid first-hand account of the dangers and hardships experienced by the troops stationed there to guard the Hittite frontier against an Egyptian attack. The account is provided in a letter, discovered in Ugarit in 1956, written by the field commander to the Hittite king, probably the great warrior-king Suppiluliuma I (c.1350–1322).[14] The last part of the field commander's name is lost. We know him only as Sumi[-]. He and his troops had already spent five months on active duty in the field as front-line forces. Their task was to defend the strategically important frontier region in southern Amurru, between Mt Lebanon and the sea, against incursions by Egyptian forces. Tensions in the region were high, for Egypt was determined to regain control of Amurrite territory, which it had lost to Hatti when its local ruler Aziru had switched his allegiance from the pharaoh Akhenaten to Suppiluliuma.

Time and again, Sumi[-]'s men had fought off attacks by the Egyptian forces. In the process, they had sustained heavy casualties, and now harsh winter conditions were causing additional casualties and imposing further severe hardships. Several times Sumi[-] wrote to his king, urgently requesting reinforcements and fresh supplies, but there had apparently been no response. Again he wrote, his letter betraying his growing sense of despair: 'My Lord, what is my outlet from here? Now for five months the cold has been gnawing me, my chariots are broken, my horses are dead, and my troops are lost!'[15]

In a series of night attacks, the enemy finally succeeded in breaching the Hittite defences and bursting into the garrison's fortress, where there was hand-to-hand fighing. The Hittites finally repulsed the enemy assault, but it took all their reserves of energy to do so: 'My men were attacked repeatedly in the middle of the night, and a battle was waged between them. My men drove them out, and heaped up their equipment and their

---

14. S. S. Izre'el and I. Singer, *The General's Letter from Ugarit* (Tel Aviv, 1990).
15. This text and the following translated passages from the letter are adapted from Singer's translation.

The Yerkapı rampart appears to have formed part of Hattusa's fortification system in the south. Staircases led from the ground to the top. There are a number of practical reasons for believing the rampart was not intended to strengthen Hattusa's defences so much as to serve as an architectural monument to the city's might and splendour.

property. It was within the fortress itself that they were fighting.' The garrison had stood its ground, but the crisis was far from over. One of the enemy was taken prisoner, and under interrogation revealed an alarming piece of news: the pharaoh himself was preparing to come to the region. Almost certainly this meant a major Egyptian campaign was being planned, under the pharaoh's personal command. If that happened, there was no way Sumi[-] could hold the line, with a seriously depleted contingent of exhausted troops, against the full might of a well-equipped Egyptian army under the command of the pharaoh himself. Sumi[-] could only hope that the prisoner had given a false report, or that the pharaoh would send only an expeditionary force. He could deal with that – but only if reinforcements were sent to him: 'May the king assign troops and chariots, so that we can fight against them and overpower them by force.' A decisive showdown was the only way to ensure that 'once and for all my enemies will be annihilated.'

Unfortunately we do not know the outcome of this episode. But we do know that around this time Akhenaten died, plunging his kingdom into crisis, for there was only a nine-year-old child called Tutankhamun to succeed him. Perhaps then, the pressure on Hatti's southern frontier eased, and, hopefully, the garrison was brought up to full strength and reprovisioned.

Regions that were considered vulnerable in the homeland itself were always protected by Hittite militias. In these regions, Hittite kings established a number of frontier settlements, basically military outposts defended by a garrison and placed under the command of an official called the *BEL MADGALTI*, an expression that means 'Lord of the Watch-Tower'. *BEL MADGALTI* was the term used for border commanders or district governors, who were officials placed in charge of outlying regions of the kingdom. They had administrative duties, which included managing the king's lands in the region and collecting his taxes, and judicial

responsibilities, which entailed travelling around their district to preside at local assizes. They were responsible for the maintenance of buildings, roads and irrigation canals, for which, very likely, labour was largely supplied by the troops stationed in the area.

The security of the region over which they exercised authority, however, was their most important responsibility. In accordance with this responsibility, they had to make sure that fortresses and towns in the region were securely locked in the evenings, that an adequate supply of timber was kept on hand in case of siege, and that all precautions were taken against the outbreak of fire. They were also responsible for arranging a careful scrutiny of all those who left the fortified community in the morning, probably mainly peasant farmers, and returned in the evening after working in the fields. The scrutiny was intended to ensure there were no enemy infiltrators among the workers.

All these responsibilities highlight the emphasis that the Hittites placed on exercising constant vigilance, both in the urban centres as well as in the outlying districts of the kingdom. Sentry duty and patrols were among the troops' most important duties. Some of the soldiers were assigned guard duty at various places within the city and along its walls. Others were sent out to man the watch-towers that were built at regular intervals between those settlements located in regions near the frontiers. Any suspicious activity was immediately reported to the local commander. The watch-tower contingent was divided into day and night shifts. Those returning from their shift at the end of the day brought back into the city with them the inhabitants of the city, and their livestock, who had spent the day in the fields. Another group called 'watchmen of the long roads' were sent out to guard the main roads between the settlements, and to conduct reconnaissance patrols into enemy territory, to check on suspicious enemy activity in the frontier region. If the patrols or watch-tower sentries reported that the enemy had crossed into Hittite territory, all the region's inhabitants were kept within the city's locked gates until an expeditionary force had driven the intruders back into their own territory, or sentries posted at appropriate vantage points reported that the enemy had of their own accord returned to their own territory.

When all the inhabitants of the settlement were safely inside for the night, the bronze-sheathed wooden gates were swung shut, and copper bolts were inserted and sealed with the stamp of the authorized officer. Once the settlement's gates had been bolted and sealed, an added precaution was taken against a secret infiltration or surprise enemy attack by assigning a number of soldiers to bunk down for the night immediately inside the gatehouses. It would thus have been impossible for any intruders to enter the city through the gates without alerting the soldiers sleeping there, for the gates opened inwards. The following morning, sentries checked the horizon carefully to ensure, once more, that there were no enemy groups in the area. When the all-clear had been given, the seal of the gate was inspected to confirm that it had not been tampered with, and then broken so that the bolts could be removed and the gates opened. The settlement's inhabitants could now safely return to their fields.

Frontier settlements played a vital role in the security of the Hittite homeland – particularly those located in the northern part of the homeland, which was especially vulnerable to raiding expeditions and sometimes full-scale invasions by the Kaskan tribes. Left unchecked, these peoples could sweep through the Hatti land, destroying everything in their path. In fact, much of the northern part of the homeland was for many years left in a ruined, abandoned state because of Kaskan raids. From the late 14th century onwards, however, Hittite kings instituted a

Hittite frontier defence settlement. This is a reconstruction of the Hittite town called Sarissa. Lying 200km (124 miles) to the south-east of Hattusa, it was a well-fortified frontier city of medium size, covering an area of 18 hectares (44.5 acres). (Courtesy A Müller-Karpe)

Troops marching through a garrison town. Though set up primarily for military purposes, many of these towns developed the character of small urban centres, with markets and various other attractions associated with larger cities. (Courtesy Ekip Film)

repopulation programme, rebuilding the ruined and abandoned cities, and putting back in them the descendants of the original inhabitants, bolstered by new settlers, who included groups of transportees. The repopulation programme provided an important buffer for the core territory of the Hittite homeland against enemy incursions. Hence the emphasis on ensuring that the inhabitants were adequately defended, and that the troops assigned to their defence remained on a high state of alert.

The king kept a close interest in the security of these regions, constantly sending written instructions to his frontier commanders and receiving regular bulletins from them in return. Many of these bulletins have survived and provide us with one of our most important sources of information on the defence of the realm. They contain demands from the king for constant updates on enemy movements; they provide his responses to local governors' requests for auxiliary troops to strengthen the existing defence forces; they issue the king's instructions regarding the relocation of populations in territories threatened by the enemy; they stipulate the treatment to be accorded to defectors and enemy prisoners who had surrendered or been taken in battle. The bulletins are terse and to the point: 'Thus His Majesty: Say to Kassu [the military commander for the region]: "Regarding what you have written to me on the matter of the chariots, note this: I have now sent forth the chariots. Look out for them!"'[16]

16. This text and the following extracts are from the Masat/Tapikka letters; see Bryce, *Letters*, pp.171–81.

Despite reports of military successes by frontier commanders against the enemies, other reports make clear how fragile Hittite security often was in these regions. It was virtually impossible to provide a complete defence against the hit-and-run raids into Hittite territory at which the Kaskan tribesmen were so skilful. 'In two places the enemy has crossed the frontiers in great numbers', a frontier official informs the king. Raids on cattle and crops were a further problem. A bulletin from the commanding officer in a frontier town called Kasepura reports to the king: 'The enemy marched in great numbers in the night, in one place 600 enemy, in another place 400 enemy, and harvested the grain.' Enemy raids on food-producing lands could have had the most serious consequences, for the homeland was highly dependent on these territories. It was vital that the agricultural produce of the state be secured against the enemy, at all costs.

Outbreaks of fever and plague were yet further hazards faced by the local population. The worst recorded plague of all was brought back to the Hatti land by Egyptian prisoners-of-war in the aftermath of a successful Hittite expedition into Egyptian territory in southern Syria. The plague carried off the great Hittite king Suppiluliuma and his son and first successor Arnuwanda. It ravaged the Hittite homeland and decimated its population for some 20 years before it finally abated.

Undoubtedly, life in the frontier settlements could be hard for soldier and civilian alike. We should also stress that these settlements were not merely military outposts. They were fully fledged townships with temples and no doubt many of the amenities of life enjoyed by inhabitants in the larger cities. The defence force was probably of mixed origin, made up partly of regular professional troops, partly of troops levied from provincial regions, partly of transportees from conquered territories now conscripted into the king's militia, and partly of called-up reservists and civilians. Troops in the last two categories may have played a particularly important role in frontier defence at times when permanent troops were recalled for military campaigns elsewhere during the campaigning season.

Leisure activities

If life was hard in these settlements, each of them no doubt provided diversions for the troops when they were not on duty. Games and athletics contests were a prominent feature of the kingdom's religious festivals, and the obvious popularity of sport in the Hittite world was very likely reflected in the leisure activities of the troops. Wrestling, weight-lifting competitions, foot races, horse races, archery contests and mock battles probably occupied much of their leisure time. All these activities figured in the festival programmes. No doubt the major festivals were as enthusiastically celebrated in the frontier towns as they were in the capital and other major cities. Though essentially religious in nature, the festivals provided occasions for feasting and entertainment.

Of course, no frontier town, especially one with a large military population, would have been complete without its taverns. Unfortunately, we have little information about these – which is only to be expected, since the kingdom's official archives are hardly likely to go into the details of what went on in the local drinking houses. One of our texts mentions 'hostels behind the Kaskan towns'. These were almost certainly drinking houses patronized by the local frontier populations – particularly Hittite

Relief sculpture from the walls of the Hittite city Alaca Höyük, depicting acrobats and a sword-swallower. Though this particular sculpture may represent part of a religious festival, it almost certainly depicts the kind of diversions enjoyed by Hittite troops as well as other members of the population.

warriors, since they appear to have been built outside the townships. The towns were thus spared much of the noise and brawling regularly associated with such establishments, and particularly at night few other than armed men would have risked leaving the security of the city for the joys of the tavern.

The texts also refer to an establishment called an *arzana* house where food and drink were consumed, musical entertainment provided, guests sang songs and overnight accommodation was available. It is possible that the proprietors of such establishments were women, as was the case in apparently similar establishments in Babylonia. The *arzana* houses were used by high-class clientele on occasions, and for certain religious rituals, such as the induction of a Hittite prince, on reaching puberty, into his first sexual experience, using the services of a group of prostitutes for the purpose. The fact that this particular ritual was conducted in this type of establishment very likely indicates the nature of the entertainment provided by the establishment on secular occasions, and probably for clientele belonging to a lower order of society, especially rank-and-file soldiers. Sometimes these establishments were built against the city wall, a practice that the local commanders were ordered to ban. The reason may have been that such places were prone to being burnt down, albeit accidentally, by drunken revellers. That, perhaps, was one of the major reasons why soldiers' drinking houses, with all their associated entertainment, were often built at some distance outside the walls.

SITES, MUSEUMS AND ELECTRONIC SOURCES

The Hittites have left us with relatively few remains of their material civilization. By far the most prominent archaeological site is the Hittite capital Hattusa in central Turkey, about 160km (100 miles) east of Ankara near the modern village called Boghazköy or Boghazkale. The city's walls encompass an area of about 162 hectares (400 acres). Though now in a very ruined state, there are still significant remains of the Late Bronze Age city. These include the city's three main gates, identified today by their sculptures – the Lion, Sphinx and 'King's' gates. Large parts of the city's southern fortifications survive, including a postern tunnel and an impressive stone rampart with staircases leading to the summit. The northern or so-called 'lower city' contains Hattusa's royal acropolis, where the foundations of palace buildings can still be seen. Close to the acropolis lies the massive Temple of the Storm God, the Hittites' greatest architectural achievement, covering an area of 20,000 sq.m (23,900 sq.yards). Hattusa has been under almost continuous excavation by German archaeological teams since the early 20th century. Discoveries in recent times include 26 temples (bringing the total number of known temples in the city to 31), two sets of large granaries, sacred pools and a building now referred to as the 'Südburg structure', probably a symbolic entrance to the Underworld. Dating to the last years of the Bronze Age, this building is embellished with reliefs and a hieroglyphic inscription composed by the last known Hittite king, Suppiluliuma II. It provides valuable information about the kingdom's final years. Recently, a large section of Hattusa's fortifications has been reconstructed to its original height. It is one of the highlights of a visit to the site today.

The progress of the ongoing excavations at Hattusa can be followed by visiting the Hattusa Project Internet site: www.hattuscha.de.

Just to the east of Hattusa lies the open-air rock sanctuary now known as Yazılıkaya, the Turkish name for 'Inscribed Rock'. Its two natural rock chambers, fronted by a temple, are embellished with processions of gods and a unique relief of a 'dagger god' plunged into the ground. The Hittite king Tudhaliya IV is also depicted, on one occasion in the embrace of his patron god Sharrumma. Almost certainly he commissioned the reliefs.

A distance of 24km (15 miles) north of Hattusa lies what was probably one of the most important holy cities of the Hittite world. Its ancient name may have been Arinna, but today the site is called Alaca Höyük. The splendid array of artefacts unearthed from 13 'royal' shaft graves of the Early Bronze Age are now on display in a number of museums, mostly in the archaeological museum in Ankara. The most impressive remains of the Late Bronze Age Hittite city are a series of sculptured orthostats (upright stone slabs), which form part of the monumental entrance to the city.

Hattusa fortifications. This picture shows a recently reconstructed section of Hattusa's walls. The city's most extensive fortifications may date to the 13th century BC, i.e. the last century of the kingdom's existence. (Courtesy Deutsches Archäologische Institut – Istanbul)

A dagger god from Yazılıkaya. The relief depicts a dagger or sword plunged into the ground. Its hilt consists of the head and shoulders of a god, with two lions' pelts below. The lower part of the relief is in the form of a double-edged blade with a distinct midrib, only the top half of which is visible.

The reliefs depict a religious festival in progress. There are representations of the king and queen standing before an altar of the Storm God, zoomorphically represented as a bull, a seated goddess (almost certainly the Sun Goddess), cult officials and animals for sacrifice, a sword-swallower, acrobats, a lute-player and perhaps a bagpiper. The entrance is flanked by two colossal sphinxes.

Other sites of the Hittite world include three provincial administrative centres, discovered in comparatively recent times. These are the cities called Sapinuwa (modern Ortaköy), Sarissa (modern Kusakli) and Tapikka (modern Masat). All have produced tablet archives (from Sapinuwa more than 3,000 have come to light) that provide valuable information on the life and sometimes hazardous existence of communities in the peripheral areas of the Hittite homeland.

Hittite relief and freestanding sculptures, tablets and stamp-seals with cuneiform and hieroglyphic inscriptions, ceramic ware, weapons, tools, domestic utensils and ritual objects are distributed among many museums, including the British Museum, the Ashmolean Museum (Oxford, UK), the Louvre, the Oriental Institute of the University of Chicago, the Metropolitan Museum of Art, New York, and the archaeological museum in Istanbul. But by far the finest collection of Hittite material is to be found in the Museum of Ancient Anatolian Civilizations in Ankara. This museum has a superb assemblage of Hittite remains as well as material from other ancient Anatolian civilizations. The museum at Boghazköy, near the Hittite capital, contains some of the most recent discoveries from Hattusa. It should certainly be included in a visit to Hattusa.

The Hittites have featured in a number of television documentaries, including Michael Wood's *In Search of the Trojan War*, by the British Broadcasting Corporation (BBC), and the BBC's later film *The Truth of Troy*. It has also recently completed a documentary on the Hittites entitled *The Dark Lords of Hattusha*. Directed by Martin Wilson, it contains excellent dramatic re-enactments and computer-generated reconstructions of the Hittite capital, and reflects up-to-date research on the Hittites themselves, especially in their final years. The most comprehensive treatment of the Hittites on film is the Turkish-American production *The Hittites*, directed by Tolga Örnek of Ekip Film. The docu-drama ranges over almost 500 years of Hittite history from its rise in the 17th century to its collapse early in the 12th century BC. Filming was done on 36 archaeological sites in Turkey, Syria and Egypt. Fifteen international experts were involved in the project. The film provides excellent material for students and anyone else wishing to explore further the history and civilization of the Hittites. For DVDs of the film, see the website www.ekipfilm.com.

BIBLIOGRAPHY

Akurgal, E., *The Art of the Hittites* (London, 1962)

Alp, S., *Hethitische Briefe aus Masat-Höyük* (Ankara, 1991)

Beal, R. H., *The Organization of the Hittite Military* (Heidelberg, 1992)

– 'Hittite Military Organization', in Sasson (ed.), *Civilizations*, pp.545–54.

Beckman, G., 'The Siege of Uršu Text (CTH 7) and Old Hittite Historiography', *Journal of Cuneiform Studies*, 47 (1995), pp.23–34

– *Hittite Diplomatic Texts*, 2nd edn (Atlanta, 1999)

Bittel, K., *Die Hethiter* (Munich, 1976)

Bryce, T. R., 'Madduwatta and Hittite Policy in Western Anatolia', *Historia*, 35 (1986), pp.1–12

– *Life and Society in the Hittite World* (Oxford, 2002)

– *Letters of the Great Kings of the Ancient Near East* (London, 2003)

– *The Kingdom of the Hittites* (Oxford, 2005)

Gardiner, A., *The Kadesh Inscriptions of Ramesses II* (Oxford, 1960, reprinted 1975)

Goetze, A., *Die Annalen des Mursilis* (Leipzig, 1933; repr. Darmstadt, 1967)

Gurney, O. R., 'The Hittite Empire', in M. T. Larsen (ed.),
    Power and Propaganda (Copenhagen, 1979), pp.151–65
– *The Hittites* (London, 1990)
Güterbock, H. G., 'The Deeds of Suppiluliuma as told by his Son,
    Mursili II', *Journal of Cuneiform Studies*, 10 (1956) pp.41–68,
    75–98, 101–30
– 'The Hittite Conquest of Cyprus Reconsidered', *Journal of Near
    Eastern Studies*, 26 (1967), pp.73–81
Hoffner, H. A., 'The *Arzana* House', in K. Bittel *et al.* (eds), *Anatolian
    Studies presented to Hans Hustav Güterbock on the Occasion of his
    65th Birthday* (Istanbul, 1974), pp.113–22
– 'The Treaty of Tudhaliya IV with Kurunta of Tarhuntassa on the
    Bronze Tablet Found in Hattusa', in W. W. Hallo and K. L. Younger
    (eds), *The Context of Scripture, Vol II: Monumental Inscriptions from the
    Biblical World* (Leiden, Boston, Cologne, 2000), pp.100–06
– 'The Treatment and Long-Term Use of Persons Captured in Battle
    according to Masat Texts', in K. A. Yener and H. A. Hoffner (eds),
    *Recent Developments in Hittite Archaeology and History, Papers in Memory
    of Hans G. Güterbock* (Winona Lake, 2002), pp.61–72
Hout, T. van den, 'Khattushili III, King of the Hittites', in Sasson (ed.),
    Civilizations, pp.1107–20
Houwink ten Cate, Ph. H. J., 'The History of Warfare according to
    Hittite Sources: The Annals of Hattusilis I (Part II)', *Anatolica*, XI
    (1984), pp.47–83
Izre'el, S. and Singer, I., *The General's Letter from Ugarit* (Tel Aviv, 1990)
Kitchen, K., *Pharaoh Triumphant: The Life and Times of Ramesses II*
    (Warminster, 1982)
Klengel, H., *Geschichte des Hethitischen Reiches* (Leiden, 1999)
– *Hattuschili und Ramses, Hethiter und Ägypter – ihr langer Weg zum Frieden*
    (Mainz am Rhein, 2002)
Liverani, M., *International Relations in the Ancient Near East, 1600–1100 BC*,
    (New York, Basingstoke, 2001)
Macqueen, J. G., *The Hittites and their Contemporaries in Asia Minor*
    (London, 1986)
– 'The History of Anatolia and of the Hittite Empire', in Sasson (ed.),
    Civilizations, pp.1085–1105
McMahon, G., 'The History of the Hittites', *Biblical Archaeologist*, 52
    (1989), pp.62–77
Murnane, W. J., *The Road to Kadesh*, 2nd edn (Chicago, 1990)
Neve, P. J., *Hattusa: Stadt der Götter und Tempel* (Mainz am Rhein, 1993)
Niemeier, W. D., 'Mycenaeans and Hittites in War in Western Asia
    Minor', *Aegaeum*, 19 (1999), pp.141–55
Nougayrol, J. *et al.*, *Ugaritica V, Mission de Ras Shamra Tome XVI*
    (Paris, 1968)
Pritchard, J. B. (ed.), *Ancient Near Eastern Texts relating to the Old
    Testament*, 3rd edn (Princeton, 1969)
Sasson, J. M. (ed.), *Civilizations of the Ancient Near East*, 4 vols
    (New York, 1995)
Seeher, J., *Hattusha Guide. A Day in the Hittite Capital* (Istanbul, 2002)
Singer, I., 'The Battle of Nihriya and the End of the Hittite Empire',
    Zeitschrift für Assyriologie und Vorderasiatische Archäologie, 75 (1985),
    pp.100–23

COLOUR PLATE COMMENTARY

A: HITTITE WARRIORS

The warriors depicted here are based on Egyptian reliefs of Hittite warriors as well as on reliefs from the Hittite world. Both are infantrymen from the ranks, though there seems to have been little to differentiate ordinary soldiers from officers in terms of the uniforms they wore. Soldiers wore their hair shoulder length, sometimes plaited, probably to help protect the backs of their necks in battle. All wore leather ankle-length boots, upturned at the toes, apparently an advantage when marching hundreds of miles over rough and stony ground. The torso was covered by a garment made of a light fabric, belted at the waist, with sleeves reaching to the wrists or just below the elbows. Its length varied from just above the knees to just above the ankles. Quite possibly, each soldier had in his kit both types of garment for use in different conditions, depending on whether he was on the march, preparing for battle, laying siege to a city or confronting an enemy in forested, rugged mountain terrain. Helmets were probably worn at all times on a campaign. They were made either of leather or bronze. A short sword or dagger was standard equipment. The infantry carried spears, 2.1–2.4m (7–8ft) in length, but perhaps only in the front ranks, for discharging at the enemy in the initial battle charge. Sentries and guards always carried spears. The battle-axe was almost certainly standard issue for all troops. Shields extending from chin to thigh were made of animal hide stretched tightly over a wooden frame. Their use may have been restricted to charioteers and front-line infantry.

B: RECRUITING SCENE

The Hittites' annual and often lengthy campaigns, sometimes in countries far from the homeland, were a constant drain on the kingdom's adult male population. So too was the dispatch of garrison forces to vulnerable frontier regions. Chronic manpower shortages led to the need for regular and comprehensive recruiting campaigns throughout the kingdom. Recruits were selected from prisoners-of-war taken from a conquered city, from the civilian population of the homeland and from levies imposed on the subject territories. This last category is depicted here. It was the responsibility of the authorities in each district to decide who the recruits would be – though slaves were banned. For many draftees taken from distant parts of the Hittite empire, life in the Hittite army could have had little appeal. Like all recruits, they faced a hard and uncertain life, torn from their families, subject to harsh discipline and to the rigours and dangers of long campaigns. All these hardships they were forced to undergo in the service of a king and a kingdom for whom they felt little or no loyalty. The only consolation was

Reconstruction of the King's Gate, one of the three main gates providing access to the Hittite royal capital. On the inner side of the gate is depicted an armed soldier, almost certainly intended to be a god equipped for war. (U. Betin after P. Neve; courtesy Deutsches Archäologische Institut – Istanbul)

that recruits from a particular area lived and fought together as a military unit, under a commander from the same area. In this plate, unwilling draftees are having their names and regions recorded by scribes, perhaps along with any skills they already possess that might be useful to the army, prior to receiving their basic uniform and equipment. It was essential to keep a record of all recruits, to ensure that desertion – which did occur and was harshly punished – was kept to a minimum.

C: HITTITE CHARIOT TRAINING

The Hittite army's elite force was its chariot contingent. Indeed, the outcome of a battle often depended very largely on the effectiveness of the chariotry. Though details have not been preserved, we know that the charioteers were obliged to undergo a rigorous training programme. This probably became even more rigorous when the Hittites changed from two-man to three-man chariots some time before the battle of Kadesh (1274). The extra man created additional challenges in ensuring that the chariot continued to be fast, stable and manoeuvrable in battle. From a Hittite horse-training manual, we can conclude that an elliptical track was marked out for the training of both horses and charioteers. Plate C shows a training session in progress. A mishap has occurred. One of the chariots has overturned, either because of driver error, or the failure of the fighter and defender to shift their weight and lean the right way at the right time, or because the vehicle's undercarriage has collapsed. This mishap also provides a useful test for the following chariot, which is fast bearing down upon the overturned vehicle. The driver of the chariot must manoeuvre around the obstacle within a very confined space, and without losing momentum or overturning his own vehicle, a situation that could frequently occur on an actual field of battle. Of course, the training programmes were as much a test of the horses and the chariots as they were of the charioteers. Horses that failed to meet the highest standards of performance and durability were culled, and the chariots themselves needed to be thoroughly tested on the training ground to ensure that they would not fall apart in battle.

D: HITTITE NIGHT ATTACK ON ENEMY CITY

Hittite infantry troops, charioteers and chariot-horses were thoroughly trained for night manoeuvres. Attacks on enemy establishments under cover of darkness often had the advantage of surprise, and enemy cities that had withstood Hittite attacks during daylight hours sometimes succumbed to a night attack. The Hittite king Hattusili I reports: 'I ascended the city of Zippasna in the dead of night. I entered into battle with its population and heaped dust upon them.' A well-fortified city could hold out for months against an army laying siege to it, and on occasions the Hittites were forced to abandon a siege or resume it in a new campaigning season. But a well-mounted shock night assault sometimes offered greater and speedier prospects of success. Here a Hittite night attack is in progress. The Hittite king, who directs operations from the safety of a nearby hill, has chosen this particular night because there is

a full moon that illuminates the city, while its attackers remain largely shrouded in darkness. Under cover of archers firing their missiles at the defenders on the walls, who are raining down fire-arrows and spears upon the attackers, a group of soldiers launch an assault on the city's main gate with an enormous wooden battering ram. The gate is a double-leaved wooden structure sheathed in bronze. A daylight assault on this gate had failed when the defenders mounted a furious counter-attack at the gate's entrance, some of them by suddenly opening and streaming through the gate brandishing swords and axes, others by charging out of the postern tunnel to the left of the main gate, catching the battering contingent and its covering archers completely off guard.

E: KINGS HARNESSED TO A BAGGAGE WAGON

This a reconstruction of a recorded historical event. After fierce resistance, the city either known as Hahha or Hahhum on the Euphrates river finally fell to the Hittite king Hattusili I (c.1650–20), who plundered it and put it to the torch: 'And I marched against Hahha and three times made battle within the gates. I destroyed Hahha and took possession of its property and carried it off to Hattusa. Two pairs of transport wagons were loaded with silver.' The defenders who had courageously fought back the Hittites in three engagements finally succumbed. A city that submitted to the Hittites without resistance was spared plunder and the slaughter of its inhabitants, but if the city had to be taken by force, no mercy was shown. Hahha/Hahhum was such a city. After looting everything of value within it, the Hittites razed it to the ground. There was one final indignity to be inflicted, however. When the baggage wagons were being laden with plunder to be taken back to Hattusa, Hattusili gave orders that the king of Hahha and the king of another conquered city, Hassuwa, should be used instead of oxen to pull one of the wagons: 'I, the Great King, destroyed Hassuwa and Hahha and burned them down with fire and showed the smoke to the Storm God of Heaven. And I harnessed the king of Hassuwa and the king of Hahha to a transport wagon.' The hapless kings are here shown harnessed to a wagon bearing the spoils of their cities. They are taunted by the soldiers escorting the baggage train.

F: THE TRANSPORTEES

As we have noted, when a city refused to surrender voluntarily to the Hittites, it was sacked and put to the torch. Many of its population, including women and children, were then transported back to the Hittite homeland as part of the spoils of war. We can only imagine the hardships that the transportees had to endure, since Hittite texts provide no details about them, except the numbers involved, which sometimes ran into the tens of thousands in the course of a campaign. Many may well have died on the journey. It was the escorting troops' responsibility, however, to ensure that casualties were kept to a minimum, since the main purpose of the transportation system was to boost the homeland's population and workforce. Thus the troops had the task of ensuring that the captive population and their livestock were adequately provisioned and protected during the march back to the Hittite homeland. Their journey often took them through a harsh and hostile environment that provided little enough sustenance for the troops themselves. It was essential to maintain steady progress, and those who fell ill or were too weak to continue were probably simply abandoned. A sentry posted on the hill in the foreground keeps a lookout for signs of a possible ambush ahead. Close vigilance also has to be maintained over the prisoners to ensure that none of them try to escape, and find refuge in a neighbouring country.

G: THE BATTLE OF KADESH

The famous battle of Kadesh, fought between the pharaoh Ramesses II and the Hittite king Muwattalli II in 1274, is one of the best-documented battles of the ancient world. An account of it and the events leading up to it are emblazoned on the walls of five Egyptian temples. Unfortunately, we have no corresponding Hittite version, and the Egyptian account is heavily biased and distorted. In spite of Ramesses' claim to have won a great victory, the battle ended in a stalemate, and the pharaoh's statement that he single-handedly destroyed all the Hittite chariotry surrounding him is clearly a gross exaggeration. Undoubtedly Ramesses fought courageously and succeeded in blunting the force of the surprise Hittite attack, but he must have had more support than he admits. Here the pharaoh is personally leading his chariot contingent into battle – as he may well have done – against an opposing Hittite chariot force. We see here the difference between the two-man Egyptian and the three-man Hittite chariot. There is no indication that the Hittites benefited in this or in any other battle from their innovation in chariot technology, though in some cases they may well have done so.

H: FRONTIER DUTY

Throughout its history, the Hittite homeland was threatened by hostile forces all around its frontiers. None of these frontiers provided any natural defences against enemy invasion or encroachment. Therefore a high degree of vigilance along the frontiers, with the establishment of garrison towns at strategic locations, was essential to the homeland's security. A series of watch-towers dotted the frontier regions. These were manned by sentries, working in shifts to ensure 24-hour coverage, whose job it was to scan the surrounding countryside for any signs of enemy movement. Sentries also manned the walls of the frontier towns, whose gates were bolted and sealed when darkness fell. When there were signs, reported by the sentries, of an enemy presence in a particular region, patrols were dispatched to scout the region. On this occasion, dawn is breaking, signifying the end of the night sentry's watch. He sees his day relief approaching from the walled garrison town in the distance. The area in which this watch-tower has been built is prone to enemy raids because of its grainfields and cattle pastures. A Hittite night patrol has in fact captured two members of a large raiding party that had slipped across the frontier during the night and begun harvesting the grain. The patrol is just leaving the watch-tower, where a small store of food and drink is kept. The soldiers have taken

The blade of a Hittite bronze axe, originally attached to a wooden handle. (Courtesy University of Queensland Antiquities Museum)

refreshments there before escorting their prisoners back to the garrison town. They will make a report to the garrison commander, who will in turn send an urgent bulletin to the king in Hattusa, informing him of the raid and urging him to send extra troops to the region, to prevent such raids in the future.

INDEX

References to illustrations are shown in **bold**.
Plates are shown with page and caption locators
in brackets.